SpringerBriefs in Law

SpringerBriefs present concise summaries of cutting-edge research and practical applications across a wide spectrum of fields. Featuring compact volumes of 50 to 125 pages, the series covers a range of content from professional to academic. Typical topics might include:

- A timely report of state-of-the art analytical techniques
- A bridge between new research results, as published in journal articles, and a contextual literature review
- A snapshot of a hot or emerging topic
- A presentation of core concepts that students must understand in order to make independent contributions

SpringerBriefs in Law showcase emerging theory, empirical research, and practical application in Law from a global author community. SpringerBriefs are characterized by fast, global electronic dissemination, standard publishing contracts, standardized manuscript preparation and formatting guidelines, and expedited production schedules.

Erich Vranes

EU Energy Politics and WTO Law

Protecting the Internal Energy Market in a WTO-Compliant Manner

Springer

Erich Vranes
Institute for European and International Law
Vienna University of Economics and Business
Wien, Austria

ISSN 2192-855X ISSN 2192-8568 (electronic)
SpringerBriefs in Law
ISBN 978-3-032-02391-9 ISBN 978-3-032-02392-6 (eBook)
https://doi.org/10.1007/978-3-032-02392-6

This Springer imprint is published by the registered company Springer Nature Switzerland AG
The registered company address is: Gewerbestrasse 11, 6330 Cham, Switzerland

Competing Interests

The author has no competing interests to declare that are relevant to the content of this manuscript.

Contents

Chapter 1
Introduction

Abstract Many states have responded to the current geopolitical uncertainties by seeking to increase their "strategic sovereignty". In the EU, this reorientation is taking place under the banners of "strategic autonomy" and, more recently, "open strategic autonomy" (OSA), where the EU is increasingly employing new forms of unilateral trade measures. What characterises the general geopolitical context also applies to the international energy landscape, which is today characterized by an unprecedented level of uncertainty. Experts have therefore urged the EU to strive for strategic sovereignty in energy matters as well. As the EU Internal Energy Market is central to this, it needs to be protected by complementary new and partly novel unilateral trade instruments. Three "horizontal instruments" have been considered to be of crucial importance in this context, namely the EU Investment Screening Regulation, the EU Carbon Border Adjustment Mechanism (CBAM) and the EU Foreign Subsidies Regulation. This study seeks to clarify the extent to which these new instruments may violate of the World Trade Organization (WTO) law. This Chapter provides a brief introduction to these issues.

We live in an age of uncertainty. This is evident in the current geopolitical context.[1]

Many states have responded to this situation by seeking to increase their "strategic sovereignty". In the EU, this reorientation is taking place under the banners of "strategic autonomy" and, more recently, "open strategic autonomy" (OSA), where the EU is increasingly employing new forms of unilateral trade measures.[2]

What characterises the general geopolitical context also holds true for the international energy landscape, which, for several years by now, has been marked by an

[1] Cf. e.g. Rodik and Walt (2022), p. 142, who e.g. refer to the rise of China, the decline of US power, the erosion of the partially liberal, rules-based system in recent years, repeated financial crises, rising inequality, renewed protectionism, the COVID-19 pandemic and growing reliance on economic sanctions. See also the other contributions to Centennial Issue of the Foreign Affairs magazine, entitled "The Age of Uncertainty" (Foreign Affairs 2022(5)).

[2] Cf. below, Chap. 2.

E. Vranes, *EU Energy Politics and WTO Law*, SpringerBriefs in Law,
https://doi.org/10.1007/978-3-032-02392-6_1

unprecedented degree of insecurity.[3] This state of affairs is attributed to a series of factors, in especially the surge in energy demand in China, India, East Asia, the Middle East and North Africa after the turn of the millennium; the advent of unconventional hydrocarbons in the United States;[4] the Russian-Ukrainian energy transit crises of 2006 and 2009, which have led to a growing perception of Russia as a geopolitical competitor[5] that treats energy as a tool in geopolitical power games;[6] and the invasion of the Crimea in 2014.[7] Moreover, the 2022 attack on Ukraine, the rapidly mounting challenges of climate change and the low level of resilience of existing energy systems are seen as additional causes for an ever more concerning outlook in the energy field.[8]

Also, the shifting role of the United States in the global energy system has significant implications for other stakeholders, particularly the European Union.[9] Although the United States had long been regarded as a key partner of European states in energy affairs (with the US-led "security community" within the International Energy Agency providing a reliable institutional framework), the unforeseen and brisk emergence of the US "unconventional hydrocarbons revolution" has resulted in the US becoming self-sufficient and less interested in energy cooperation with its European allies; at the same time, the US is seen as leveraging its dominant role in the financial sphere and the dollar to advance its foreign policy objectives.[10] This has led commentators to conclude that the idea of an "energy-economic West" no longer applies,[11] the liberal, market-oriented paradigm of the 1980s and 1990s being seen as giving way to a rise in "resource nationalism" and "energy geopolitics".[12] Therefore, just as the EU is now seeking to foster its "strategic autonomy" in its internal and external policies, it is perceived, and urged, to pursue the goal of strategic sovereignty in *energy* affairs.[13] This "strategic energy autonomy" (SEA) is defined as the "EU's capability to act in energy affairs to pursue its own goals, without endangering its own values, interests or foreign policy goals due to foreign influence".[14]

The EU tries to attain the SEA objective through decarbonizing its economy by 2050 in order both to decrease its external energy dependency on the one hand and reach its greenhouse gas emission reduction targets on the other hand.[15] Pursuing

---

[3] Szulecki and Westphal (2014), p. 39, citing the International Energy Agency (IEA (2010), p. 45).

[4] Szulecki and Westphal (2014), p. 39.

[5] Siddi and Kustova (2021), p. 1077.

[6] Du Plessis (2017), p. 2.

[7] Du Plessis (2017), p. 2.

[8] Szulecki and Westphal (2014), p. 39.

[9] On this and the following see in especially Westphal (2021), pp. 4 ff.

[10] See also Haass (2022), p. 38.

[11] Westphal (2021), p. 4.

[12] Szulecki and Westphal (2014), p. 39; Westphal (2021), p. 3; Haass (2022), p. 26.

[13] Westphal (2021), pp. 1 ff.

[14] Hancher and de Hauteclocque (2024), p. 59; see Westphal (2021), p. 2 for a similar definition.

[15] Cf. e.g EU Commission, RePowerEU Plan, COM/2022/230 final; EU, Joint Communication, EU external energy engagement in a changing world, JOIN/2022/23 final; on this and the following cf. Hancher and de Hauteclocque (2024), pp. 56 ff.

this objective raises a considerable number of important legal issues, as has been explained in a seminal article by *Hancher* and *de Hautecloque*:[16] On the one hand, the EU's capacity to act is complicated due to the division of powers in the field of energy, where competences are shared between the EU and its Member States in principle, but where the Member States nonetheless retain exclusive competence for determining their national energy mix (cf Arts. 4(2) TEU and 194(2) of the Treaty on the Functioning of the European Union (TFEU)). Yet, the EU's plan of decarbonization may have direct impacts on these national choices of energy sources. The SEA objective moreover raises difficult questions of guaranteeing access to energy sources such as bio-fuels and critical raw materials necessary in "greening" the energy sector. All of this calls for a more active external energy policy on the level of the EU, which must e.g. address the repercussions which the envisaged transitioning out of fossil fuels is bound to have on its neighbouring and supplying countries; moreover, the EU must also prepare to deal with the possibility of retaliatory measures.[17] Further, the EU will need to endeavour to exert influence on the establishment of relevant global norms and manage access of energy products and investments to its Internal Market.[18]

As pointed out by *Hancher* and *de Hautecloque*, the EU's *external* policy in the energy field certainly is essential; but "coordinated *internal* action" may even be more important, as the degree of external energy dependence of the EU is directly influenced by its Member States' internal approaches to energy transition.[19] Since the EU Internal Energy Market (IEM) is thus central to achieving strategic energy autonomy, it needs to be protected by complementary new and partly novel unilateral trade tools against undue foreign influences.[20] In this regard, *Hancher* and *de Hautecloque* refer to three "horizontal instruments" which they consider to be of crucial importance, namely the EU Investment Screening Regulation, the EU Carbon Border Adjustment Mechanism (CBAM) and the EU Foreign Subsidies Regulation.

The present study takes this view of *Hancher* and *de Hautecloque* as a starting point, trying to clarify the extent to which these new—and partly novel—instruments and their application potentially contravene the law of the World Trade Organization (WTO). The study first examines the development and relevance of the EU's new leitmotiv of Open Strategic Autonomy (Chap. 2). It next briefly outlines the need for protecting the EU Internal Energy Market (Chap. 3), before it turns to an in-depth scrutiny of these three cardinal "horizontal instruments" under relevant disciplines of WTO law (Chap. 4). Chapter 5 summarizes the conclusions of this study.

---

[16] Hancher and de Hauteclocque (2024), p. 55 ff.

[17] See also Leonard et al. (2021), p. 2, submitting that "the Green Deal is foreign policy".

[18] Hancher and de Hauteclocque (2024), pp. 56 ff.

[19] Hancher and de Hauteclocque (2024), pp. 61 and 80.

[20] Hancher and de Hauteclocque (2024), pp. 56 ff; this need for new EU trade measures in the energy context is also emphasized by Westphal (2021), p. 8.

References

Du Plessis W (2017) A liberal actor in a realist world. The European Union regulatory state and the global political economy of energy (book review). Potchefstroom Electr Law J 20:2–6. https://doi.org/10.17159/1727-3781/2017/v20n0a-1681

Haass R (2022) The dangerous decade. Foreign Aff 101(5):25–38

Hancher L, de Hauteclocque A (2024) Strategic autonomy, REPowerEU and the internal energy market: untying the Gordian Knot. Common Mark Law Rev 61(1):55–92

Leonard M, Pisani-Ferry J, Shapiro J, Tagliapietra S, Wolff G (2021) The geopolitics of the European Green Deal, Policy Contribution 04/2021, Bruegel. https://www.bruegel.org/system/files/wp_attachments/PC-04-GrenDeal-2021-1.pdf

Rodik D, Walt SM (2022) How to build a better order. Foreign Aff 101(5):142–155

Siddi M, Kustova I (2021) From a liberal to a strategic actor: the evolution of the EU's approach to international energy governance. J Eur Public Policy 28(7):1076–1094

Szulecki K, Westphal K (2014) The Cardinal Sins of European Energy Policy: nongovernance in an uncertain global landscape. Glob Policy 5 Supplement 1:38–51

Westphal K (2021) Strategic Sovereignty in Energy Affairs. Reflections on Germany and the EU's Ability to Act. SWP Comment No. 7:1–8. https://www.swp-berlin.org/publikation/strategic-sovereignty-in-energy-affairs

Chapter 2
"Open Strategic Autonomy": Developments and Relevance

Abstract In 2021, the EU Commission presented a new trade policy strategy, entitled "An Open, Sustainable and Assertive Trade Policy" in order to support the EU's Open Strategic Autonomy (OSA). OSA is intended to enhance the EU's ability to act in a way that reflects its strategic interests and values, particularly at the international level. This Chapter briefly explains why the vague OSA leitmotif has become a ubiquitous concept in EU affairs, reflecting in particular the erosion of multilateralism promoted by the "West" and the realisation that trade and energy policies are increasingly being "weaponised".

2.1 From "Strategic Autonomy" to "Strategic Energy Autonomy"

In the light of the many recent challenges in international trade, security, technological evolutions, climate change and the COVID 19 pandemic, the EU Commission presented a new trade policy strategy in 2021, entitled "An Open, Sustainable and Assertive Trade Policy".[1] This strategy is meant to support the EU's aforementioned Open Strategic Autonomy (OSA). OSA has been circumscribed by the EU Commission as "the EU's ability to make its own choices and shape the world around it through leadership and engagement, reflecting its strategic interests and values".[2] Although there are several divergent concepts of OSA in the literature,[3] this definition by the EU has become a central reference point in political and academic discussions, given that OSA is meant to serve as the new *leitmotiv* in the fields of EU external trade and EU external policy more generally.[4] This is under-

[1] EU Commission, Trade Policy Review - An Open, Sustainable and Assertive Trade Policy, COM(2021)66 final, pp. 1 ff.

[2] EU Commission, Trade Policy Review - An Open, Sustainable and Assertive Trade Policy, COM(2021)66 final, p. 4.

[3] On the variety of (similar) definitions cf. e.g. Helwig (2020), pp. 5 ff.

[4] De Ville et al. (2023), p. 28.

E. Vranes, *EU Energy Politics and WTO Law*, SpringerBriefs in Law,
https://doi.org/10.1007/978-3-032-02392-6_2

lined by the fact that achieving strategic autonomy has been hailed as the "number one goal for our generation" by *Charles Michel*, the former President of the European Council.[5]

While the EU's new trade strategy and the notion of OSA must be seen against the challenges just mentioned,[6] the concept of "strategic autonomy" can be traced back as far as to *de Gaulle's* foreign policy, where it was used to refer to the aspiration of decreasing dependency on the US.[7] In the EU context, the concept is said to have first been employed in the 1998 British-French St Malo declaration, where it was circumscribed as "capacity for autonomous action" and paved the way for the establishment of the EU's Common Security and Defence Policy (CSDP).[8]

Although "strategic autonomy" thus has firm roots in the defence field (as witnessed also by the fact that the first official EU document employing this term is the European Council Conclusions of December 2013, dealing with CSDP), the concept has rapidly been transposed to other policy areas.[9] As argued in an analysis by the EU Parliament, this development has been spurred in several phases. The first, between 2017 and 2019, was clearly marked by Brexit, increased US protectionism under the first Trump administration and the rise of China. While during this phase politicians in some Member States still had taken a critical attitude towards the idea of EU strategic autonomy, they appear to have changed their standpoint in a next phase, i.e. during the supply chain crisis triggered by of the COVID pandemic. Thus, many formerly sceptical politicians seemingly began to realize that a conciliation was needed between the competing objectives of an open economy and reduced external dependencies. This conciliation resulted in the terminological compromise that "strategic autonomy" has since then preponderantly been referred to as "*open* strategic autonomy". This is true in especially for the area of trade.[10] Lastly, the 2022 Russian attack on Ukraine has led to reinforced calls for open strategic autonomy, in particular in the energy field. Hence, every strategic autonomy analysis today is said to include *energy*.[11]

Meanwhile, the leitmotiv of "open strategic autonomy"—and increasingly current synonyms such as "strategic sovereignty", "capacity to act" and "resilience"[12]—are invoked in most EU policy areas.[13] As pointed out by *Miró*, this rapid evolution of OSA into such a ubiquitous concept mirrors the erosion of three key narratives of

---

[5] Miró (2022), p. 316.

[6] Helwig (2020), p. 4 (referring to these challenges as the most demanding environment since the end of the Cold War).

[7] Miró (2022), p. 317.

[8] Helwig and Sinkkonen (2022), p. 3; Lavery et al. (2022), pp. 59 ff.

[9] On this and the following see e.g. the illustrative analysis of Damen (2022), pp. 1 ff; for similar accounts see e.g. Helwig and Sinkkonen (2022), pp. 1 ff; Gehrke (2022), pp. 61 ff; Lavery et al. (2022), pp. 59 ff.

[10] Damen (2022), p. 3; see also Lavery et al. (2022), pp. 59 ff; Steinbach (2023), pp. 975 ff.

[11] Damen (2022), pp. 2 and 6-7; see also Hancher and de Hauteclocque (2024), p. 55 ff.

[12] Damen (2022), pp. 1 ff.

[13] Damen (2022), pp. 2 ff; Helwig (2020), pp. 4–5; Miró (2022), p. 315 ff.

the post-Maastricht period, namely rules-based multilateralism, the Washington Consensus and "the West" more generally.[14] Moreover, as indicated, OSA has clear connections to security, which in recent years tends to be understood ever more broadly, spanning from military and defence policy ("national security" in a traditional understanding) to economic security, health, environmental and other non-economic concerns.[15] As has also been stressed, economic interdependence, which for several decades had been seen as a key for establishing international peace, has increasingly come to be questioned in the current geopolitical context, where such interdependence is perceived as a potential weapon in international relations.[16]

As indicated, a crucial sector, where such "weaponized interdependence" risks occurring, is the field of *energy*.[17] This is reflected not least in the EU's recent annual Strategic Foresight Reports, all of which highlight sufficient supply with energy and energy-related critical raw materials as key OSA issues in coming decades.[18]

2.2 Legal and Political Relevance

The OSA policy, including its focus on energy, needs tools for implementation. In this regard, the EU Commission stresses two main levers, namely the Internal Market and the EU's Common Commercial Policy (CCP): thus, by conditioning access to the Internal Market, the EU will continue to try to export its interests and values to third countries (the famed "Brussels effect"[19]); on the other hand, by means of employing its CCP instruments, namely multilateral, bilateral, unilateral and increasingly also soft law tools,[20] the EU will continue to strive to influence international economic relations. In this context, it is of particular relevance that the EU can "speak with one voice" in CCP affairs due to its exclusive competence in this field.[21]

---

[14] Miró (2022), pp. 317 ff.

[15] Heath (2020), pp. 1020 ff; Lavery et al. (2022), pp. 57 ff; Reilly and Coget (2024).

[16] Gehrke (2022), pp. 61 ff; see also e.g. Meunier and Nicolaidis (2019), pp. 103 ff.

[17] Farrell and Newman (2019), pp. 43.

[18] EU Commission, 2021 Strategic Foresight Report. The EU's capacity and freedom to act, COM(2021)750 final, 1 ff, 9 ff; EU Commission, 2022 Strategic Foresight Report. Twinning the green and digital transitions in the new geopolitical context, COM(2022)289 final; EU Commission, 2023 Strategic Foresight Report. Sustainability and people's wellbeing at the heart of Europe's Open Strategic Autonomy COM(2023)376 final.

[19] See e.g. Christen et al. (2022), pp. 7 ff.

[20] Bohnert (2024).

[21] EU Commission, Trade Policy Review—An Open, Sustainable and Assertive Trade Policy, COM(2021)66 final, p. 6; see also EU Commission and High Representative of the Union for Foreign Affairs and Security Policy, Joint Communication. EU external energy engagement in a changing world, JOIN(2022)23 final.

Within this "new trade strategy", the EU has stressed six areas that it regards as essential in the medium term: a reform of the WTO; support of the transition to green energy and promotion of responsible and sustainable value chains; support of the digital transition and trade in services; strengthening the EU's regulatory influence in international regulatory cooperation; consolidating international partnerships; and reinforcing the implementation and enforcement of trade agreements as well as ensuring a "level playing field".[22]

It is under the latter rubric of "levelling the playing field" that the EU has introduced a series of unilateral measures, resulting in a remarkable policy reorientation that is often referred to as a "unilateral turn" in the EU's external economic relations.[23] These measures comprise (1) an update of the EU's Enforcement Regulation that is meant to strengthen the EU's capacity to act when international dispute settlement fora, in particular in the WTO, are blocked; (2) an adapted approach to the use of the EU's trade defence instruments; (3) screening of foreign direct investments (FDI Screening); (4) implementation of the modernized Export Control Regulation; (5) a new legal instrument to protect the EU from coercive action by third countries (the so-called Anti-Coercion Instrument); (6) a new instrument addressing distortions caused by foreign subsidies (the Foreign Subsidies Regulation); (7) an International Procurement Instrument; and (8) the exploration of options for an EU strategy for export credits.[24] Of these tools, the FDI Screening Regulation and the Foreign Subsidies Regulation will be discussed in detail below, together with CBAM, which also can be regarded as a relevant unilateral tool.[25]

This significant policy reorientation must also be seen against the background of the global shift away from multilateralism to increasing regionalism and bilateralism, which has been taking place since the first decade of the millennium,[26] and increasing unilateralism in recent years: whereas countries throughout the world had for a long period tried to extend market access through multilateral, bilateral and occasionally unilateral tools, they are now trying to *reduce* market access through unilateral measures for security and sustainability reasons, but also with a view to "levelling the playing field" vis à vis countries perceived as not playing by the rules of the WTO, in especially state-capitalist countries.[27] In this context, OSA establishes a partial, but distinct break away from guiding principles of the last decades, i.e. from decades marked by liberalism, the separation between state and market and the separation between security and economic affairs;[28] a turning away

[22] EU Commission, Trade Policy Review - An Open, Sustainable and Assertive Trade Policy, COM(2021)66 final, pp. 10 ff.

[23] Cf. e.g. De Ville et al. (2023), pp. 15 ff.

[24] EU Commission, Trade Policy Review - An Open, Sustainable and Assertive Trade Policy, COM(2021)66 final, pp. 10 ff.

[25] Erixon (2022), pp. 44 ff.

[26] See e.g. Griller et al. (2017), pp. 3 ff with further references.

[27] On this cf. e.g. Stellinger (2022), p. 6.

[28] Gehrke (2022), pp. 61 ff.

also from an era, guaranteed to a large extent by the US,[29] in which economic relations where legalized and depoliticized in especially within the WTO.[30]

In this light, OSA, as the new "*basso continuo*" of EU policy, is seen as the expression of a reinforced geopolitization of trade, a new doctrine of "qualified openness" of the EU Internal Market[31] and the "most significant challenge to and departure from [...] neoliberal ideas of open(-ing) markets so far", giving the EU a new direction that is not about "internal *de*bordering", but "external *re*bordering".[32]

It is rightly stressed, however, that OSA as a concept is vague, not least due to its aforementioned compromise nature, which is meant to terminologically reconcile the competing objectives of an "open" Internal Market on the one hand and intensified protection of EU interests and its "strategic autonomy" on the other. This vagueness, however, has also been regarded as "constructive ambiguity" that serves as a potential "coalition magnet" which keeps each one hoping,[33] while hiding fundamental underlying tensions.[34] As has also been observed, this strategic reorientation has the consequence that "[o]penness remains the default, but increasingly needs to be justified in terms of its contribution to autonomy".[35] This relationship between rule and exception is caught by the conclusion that "the goal is still to have as open markets *as possible*, while preserving sufficient autonomy for EU policy choices *where necessary*".[36]

In legal terms, the OSA-induced reorientation of the EU trade policy does not *per se* risk violating relevant principles in the EU treaties (such as Arts. 3(5) and 21 of the TEU or Art. 207 of the TFEU), given that the constitutional objectives and constraints expressed in these provisions leave considerable leeway to the EU legislator when adopting unilateral measures.[37] Hence, a legal assessment of OSA under EU primary law depends on its concrete implementation in secondary law and its application in concrete cases.[38] However, in the balancing of the EU's constitutional objectives[39] called for by the OSA concept, geopolitical considerations are likely to be given greater weight from now on, which is likely to result in the adoption of

---

29 Ikenberry (2018), pp. 2 ff, 14 ff.

30 Gehrke (2022), p. 64.

31 Schmitz and Seidl (2023), p. 834.

32 Schmitz and Seidl (2023), p. 836, citing Schimmelfennig (2021), p. 321; see also De Ville et al. (2023), pp. 15 ff.

33 Schmitz and Seidl (2023), pp. 836, 838.

34 Steinbach (2023), pp. 977 ff; Schmitz and Seidl (2023), pp. 834 ff.

35 Schmitz and Seidl (2023), p. 849; see also De Ville et al. (2023), pp. 15 ff.

36 De Ville et al. (2023), p. 28 (italics added); Schmitz and Seidl 834; Kübek and Mancini (2023), p. 519.

37 Kübek and Mancini (2023), p. 521.

38 On this see also Steinbach (2023), pp. 975 ff.

39 According to Art. 21(1) first subparagraph of the TEU,

> [t]he Union's action on the international scene shall be guided by the principles which have inspired its own creation, development and enlargement, and which it seeks to advance in the wider world: democracy, the rule of law, the universality and indivisibility of human

more unilateral measures in areas such as the CCP, CFSP and development policy, as well as the EU's external energy policy.[40]

References

Bohnert S (2024) The Growing "Informalisation" of EU Trade and Investment Law: The End of a Rules-Based Order? CELIS Institute Blog 18 September 2024. https://www.celis.institute/tag/soft-law/

Christen E, Meyer B, Oberhofer H, Hinz J, Kamin K, Wanner J (2022) The Brussels Effect 2.0. How the EU Sets Global Standards with its Trade Policy. FIW-Research Reports October 2022, Number 07. https://fiw.ac.at/wp-content/uploads/2023/02/FIW_RR_07_2022_Brussels-Effect.pdf

Damen M (2022) EU strategic autonomy 2013-2023. From concept to capacity. Briefing. EU Strategic Autonomy Monitor, July 2022. European Parliamentary Research Service PE 733.589.https://www.europarl.europa.eu/RegData/etudes/BRIE/2022/733589/EPRS_BRI(2022)733589_EN.pdf

De Ville F, Happersberger S, Kalimo H (2023) The unilateral turn in EU trade policy? The origins and characteristics of the EU's new trade instruments. Eur Foreign Aff Rev 28(Special Issue):15–34

---

rights and fundamental freedoms, respect for human dignity, the principles of equality and solidarity, and respect for the principles of the United Nations Charter and international law.

Art. 21(1) second paragraph emphasizes that the EU "shall promote *multilateral* solutions to common problems" (italics added).

Art. 21(2) lists further principles and objectives. Accordingly,

> [t]he Union shall define and pursue common policies and actions, and shall work for a high degree of cooperation in all fields of international relations, in order to:

(a) safeguard its values, fundamental interests, security, independence and integrity;
(b) consolidate and support democracy, the rule of law, human rights and the principles of international law;
(c) preserve peace, prevent conflicts and strengthen international security, in accordance with the purposes and principles of the United Nations Charter, with the principles of the Helsinki Final Act and with the aims of the Charter of Paris, including those relating to external borders;
(d) foster the sustainable economic, social and environmental development of developing countries, with the primary aim of eradicating poverty;
(e) encourage the integration of all countries into the world economy, including through the progressive abolition of restrictions on international trade;
(f) help develop international measures to preserve and improve the quality of the environment and the sustainable management of global natural resources, in order to ensure sustainable development;
(g) assist populations, countries and regions confronting natural or man-made disasters; and (h) promote an international system based on stronger multilateral cooperation and good global governance.

[40] Hoffmeister (2023), pp. 667 ff; see also Kübek and Mancini (2023), p. 519; Steinbach (2023), pp. 973; Schmitz and Seidl (2023), p. 834, 847; De Ville et al. (2023), p. 28.

Erixon F (2022) The new wave of defensive trade policy measures in the European Union: design, structure, and trade effects. ECIPE OCCASIONAL PAPER 04/2022. https://ecipe.org/wp-content/uploads/2022/05/ECI_22_OccPaper_Defence_04_2022_LY10.pdf
Farrell H, Newman AL (2019) Weaponized interdependence: how global economic networks shape state coercion. Int Secur 44(1):42–79
Gehrke T (2022) EU open strategic autonomy and the trappings of geoeconomics. Eur Foreign Aff Rev 27 (Special Issue):61–78
Griller S, Obwexer W, Vranes E (2017) Mega-regional agreements: CETA, TTIP, TiSA. New orientations for EU external relations? In: Obwexer W, Vranes E (eds) Griller S, Mega-regional agreements: CETA, TTIP, TiSA. New orientations for EU external economic relations. Oxford University Press, Oxford, pp 3–17
Hancher L, de Hauteclocque A (2024) Strategic autonomy, REPowerEU and the internal energy market: untying the Gordian Knot. Common Mark Law Rev 61(1): 55–92
Heath JB (2020) The new national security challenge to the economic order. Yale Law J 129:1020–1098
Helwig N (2020) EU Strategic Autonomy. A Reality Check. FIIA Working Paper 119. https://www.fiia.fi/wp-content/uploads/2020/10/wp119_strategic_autonomy-2.pdf
Helwig N, Sinkkonen V (2022) Strategic autonomy and the EU as a global actor: the evolution, debate and theory of a contested term. Eur Foreign Aff Rev 27(Special Issue):1–20
Hoffmeister F (2023) Strategic autonomy in the European Union's external relations law. Common Mark Law Rev 60(3):667–700
Ikenberry GJ (2018) The end of liberal international order? The end of liberal international order? Int Aff 94(1):7–23
Kübek G, Mancini I (2023) EU trade policy between constitutional openness and strategic autonomy. Eur Const Law Rev 19:518–547
Lavery S, McDaniel S, Schmid D (2022) European strategic autonomy: new agenda, old constraints. In: babić m, Dixon AD, Liu IT (eds) The political economy of geoeconomics: Europe in a changing world. Springer Nature, Cham, Switzerland, pp 57–80
Meunier S, Nicolaidis K (2019) The geopoliticization of European trade and investment policy. J Common Mark Stud 57(1):103–113
Miró J (2022) Responding to the global disorder: the EU's quest for open strategic autonomy. Glob Soc 37(3):315–335
Reilly T, Coget M (2024) The European Economic Security Package. Covington & Burling Global Policy Watch. https://www.globalpolicywatch.com/2024/01/the-european-economic-security-package/
Schimmelfennig F (2021) Rebordering Europe: external boundaries and integration in the European Union. J Eur Public Policy 28(3):311–330
Schmitz L, Seidl T (2023) As open as possible, as autonomous as necessary: understanding the rise of open strategic autonomy in EU trade policy. J Common Mark Stud 61(3):834–852
Steinbach A (2023) The EU's turn to 'Strategic Autonomy': Leeway for policy action and points of conflict. Eur J Int Law 34(4):973–1006
Stellinger A (2022) Preface. In: Erixon F et al (eds) The new wave of defensive trade policy measures in the European Union: design, structure, and trade effects. ECIPE OCCASIONAL PAPER 04/2022, 6. https://ecipe.org/wp-content/uploads/2022/05/ECI_22_OccPaper_Defence_04_2022_LY10.pdf

Chapter 3
The Internal Energy Market and Its Need for Protection

Abstract This short Chapter recalls that energy has been at the heart of European integration from the very beginning, as the EU integration process was started with the creation of the European Coal and Steel Community (ECSC) and the European Atomic Energy Community (Euratom). This Chapter in particular refers to a previous study which, on the one hand, emphasized that today the EU's Internal Energy Market is central to the pursuit of the EU's goal of strategic energy autonomy and, on the other hand, underlined that the EU's Investment Screening Regulation, the EU's CBAM mechanism, and the EU's Foreign Subsidies Regulation are crucial to the protection of the EU's Internal Energy Market. This Chapter thus in particular serves as a brief introduction to the following core chapter of this study, which will examine the extent to which these instruments are compatible with WTO law.

It is obvious that energy—in the form of coal, steel and nuclear power—has been at the heart of European integration from the very beginning, given that the EU integration process was started with the creation of the European Coal and Steel Community (ECSC) and the European Atomic Energy Community (Euratom).[1] However, due to the political sensitivities of energy, the goal of establishing a comprehensive Internal Energy Market (IEM) has only been vigorously pursued since the 1990s. Since then, several consecutive "Energy Packages" have been enacted to create the IEM.[2] Additionally, the political vision of an "Energy Union" was introduced in 2014 in order to promote the goals of energy security, sustainability and competitiveness.[3] Its five relevant "guiding dimensions" comprise energy security, solidarity and trust; a fully integrated European energy market; energy efficiency; decarbonization of the economy; as well as research, innovation and

[1] On this and the following cf. in particular Talus and Aalto (2017), pp. 15 ff; Winkler, Baumgart and Ackermann (2021), pp. 23 ff; see also Storr (2022), paragraphs 2.32 ff.

[2] On this see also the contributions in Jones and Kettlewell (2021).

[3] Winkler et al. (2021), p. 33.

E. Vranes, *EU Energy Politics and WTO Law*, SpringerBriefs in Law,
https://doi.org/10.1007/978-3-032-02392-6_3

competitiveness.[4] Hence, these goals visibly overlap with the aforementioned EU objective of strategic energy autonomy.

As pointed out by *Hancher* and *de Hautecloque*, the IEM can contribute to the goal of strategic energy autonomy in three ways at least: by reinforcing the competitiveness of EU industries essential for energy transition, by optimizing cross-border energy flows, and by helping to pursue decarbonization in the EU at best cost (which includes e.g. ensuring non-discriminatory market and grid access for producers of renewable energy sources as well as developing and interconnecting networks). In this regard, they also emphasize the need for new regulatory tools which are required to protect the IEM in today's geopolitical context. These tools are, first, measures necessary to control the influx of third-country FDI into relevant EU industries and infrastructure; secondly, measures guaranteeing fair competition for EU companies vis à vis competitors from third countries, in particular undertakings profiting from foreign subsidies; and, thirdly, instruments preventing the risk of EU undertakings relocating to third countries (the so-called "carbon leakage").[5]

The *corresponding horizontal unilateral tools* that are regarded as crucial for addressing *these three challenges* are (i) the EU's Investment Screening Regulation, (ii) the EU's CBAM mechanism, and (iii) the EU's Foreign Subsidies Regulation. In the next Sections, we will take examine these three instruments, focussing on the question of the extent to which these instruments and their possible application comply with the disciplines of WTO law.

References

Hancher L, de Hauteclocque A (2024) Strategic autonomy, REPowerEU and the internal energy market: untying the Gordian Knot. Common Mark Law Rev 61(1):55–92

Jones J, Kettlewell W-J (eds) (2021) EU Energy Law, 5th edn. Edward Elgar, Cheltenham, UK

Storr S (2022) Energierecht. Eine Einführung für Ausbildung und Praxis. Manz, Vienna, Austria

Talus K, Aalto P (2017) Competences in EU energy policy. In: Leal-Arcas R, Wouters J (eds) Handbook on EU energy law and policy. Edward Elgar, Cheltenham, UK, pp 15–29

Winkler D, Baumgart M, Ackermann T (2021) Europäisches Energierecht. Nomos, Baden-Baden, Deutschland

[4] Talus and Aalto (2017), pp. 17.

[5] Hancher and de Hauteclocque (2024), pp. 82 ff.

Chapter 4
Protecting the Internal Energy Market in a WTO-Consistent Manner

Abstract This Chapter examines in detail three mechanisms that have been considered crucial to the protection of the EU's Internal Energy Market and the pursuit of the EU's goal of strategic energy autonomy, namely the EU Investment Screening Regulation, the EU CBAM mechanism, and the EU Foreign Subsidies Regulation. This Chapter shows that these instruments risk violating core disciplines of WTO law that are laid down in the GATT, the GATS and the Agreement on Subsidies and Countervailing Measures (ASCM). The analysis also examines whether these instruments could be justified under the general exceptions and security exceptions clauses of the GATT and GATS.

4.1 EU Investment Screening and WTO Law

The first of the aforementioned horizontal instruments that are necessary to protect the EU's Internal Energy Market is the EU Investment Screening Regulation. This Chapter briefly explains the relevance of investment screening in the energy sector (Sect. 4.1.1), before it outlines the EU Investment Screening Regulation (Sect. 4.1.2). It then examines to what extent this regulation risks violating fundamental WTO disciplines and whether any prima facie violations of WTO rules could be justified under the general and security exceptions of the General Agreement on Tariffs and Trade (GATT) and the General Agreement on Trade in Services (GATS) (Sect. 4.1.3).

E. Vranes, *EU Energy Politics and WTO Law*, SpringerBriefs in Law,
https://doi.org/10.1007/978-3-032-02392-6_4

4.1.1 Investment Screening in the Energy Sector

In recent years, there has been a distinct intensification in the use of existing, and the introduction of new, investment screening mechanisms around the world.[1] These are employed by states as instruments to analyse foreign investment transactions, which may lead to the imposition of preconditions for, or a denial of, entry of FDI, if a given investment is deemed unacceptable by the host country.[2]

This increasing use of investment screening is particularly discernible in the *energy sector* as well. While many states have imposed numerous *sector-specific* restrictions on FDI—such as limits on shareholdings, monopolies and licensing requirements—in the energy area since the 1970s at least and while these restrictions have typically been applied to the exploration, production and supply of energy as well as to protect the energy infrastructure, there is a new tendency to apply *cross-sectoral* screening mechanisms like the EU Screening Regulation[3] to the field of energy and to extend their reach to new segments of the energy value chain such as the development of new energy technologies and data processing.[4] Moreover, key notions like critical energy infrastructure tend to be expanded; also, national screening activities have apparently become more interventionist, as is witnessed in a comparative perspective by an increasing number of prohibitions on FDI in the energy sector.[5] Nonetheless, as has been pointed out in the literature, the relationship between cross-sectoral investment screening mechanisms, such as the EU Screening Regulation, and the *energy sector* has so far remained underexplored.[6]

Likewise, despite the considerable effects that investment screening may have on international investment and trade, there is hardly any literature examining the constraints following from the legal framework of the World Trade Organization (WTO) for the design and application of investment screening mechanisms.[7] However, the importance of WTO law for such instruments is substantial: thus, the scopes of

[1] This subsection and the following draw on Vranes (2023), pp. 5 ff and 9 ff.

[2] Cf. Bauerle Danzman and Meunier (2021), p. 1; see also Voon and Merriman (2022), pp. 1 ff for a similar definition; the EU Screening Regulation defines "screening" as "a procedure allowing to assess, investigate, authorize, condition, prohibit or unwind foreign direct investment" (Regulation (EU) 2019/452 of the European Parliament and of the Council of 19 March 2019 establishing a framework for the screening of foreign direct investments into the Union, OJ L 79/1, 21.3.2019, p. 1–14, Art. 2 point (3)).

[3] Regulation (EU) 2019/452 of the European Parliament and of the Council of 19 March 2019 establishing a framework for the screening of foreign direct investments into the Union, OJ L 79/1, 21.3.2019, p. 1–14 (in the following: "EU Screening Regulation").

[4] See Rajavuori and Huhta (2020), pp. 1–2; Hancher and de Hauteclocque (2024), pp. 83 ff.

[5] Rajavuori and Huhta (2020), pp. 1 ff.

[6] Rajavuori and Huhta (2020), p. 2.

[7] There are only some notable exceptions: Fassion and Natens (2020), pp. 121 ff outline the impact of the GATT, GATS and TRIMs agreements for EU investment screening; Velten (2020), pp. 3 ff examines the relevance of the WTO concepts of security interests and public order (to be found in the general exceptions and security exceptions clauses of the GATT and GATS) for the EU Investment Screening Regulation. On these issues see in particular below, Sect. 4.1.3.4.

application of the GATT and the GATS as two of the WTO agreements primarily relevant for investment screening are broad, as they in principle apply to any measures, including measures regulating investments that—even if incidentally—*affect* trade or the "commercial presence" of foreign investors.[8]

In addition, in contrast to most bilateral investment treaties (BITs), the ambit of the GATS extends to market access obligations and, hence, the so-called pre-establishment phase of investments. Furthermore, since the scopes of the GATT and GATS overlap in several constellations, there is a clear risk that screening activities in *services* sectors where a WTO Member has not undertaken *GATS* commitments could possibly be challenged, *indirectly* under the GATT, if screening activities have the potential of affecting trade in *goods*.[9] The risk that screening mechanisms may come to be challenged before the WTO is underlined by pertinent GATT/WTO panel reports, in particular a classic GATT case involving Canadian investment screening activities (the "FIRA" case)[10] and, with respect to *energy*, the recent *EU – Energy* case, which has dealt with WTO complaints brought by Russia against the EU dealing *inter alia* with investment screening measures taken in the energy sector.[11] Although this report has not become binding due to the current crisis of the WTO Appellate Body,[12] it illustrates relevant questions in WTO law.

4.1.2 The EU Screening Regulation Outlined

The EU Screening Regulation is meant to establish a framework for the EU Member States' investment screening activities and to provide a mechanism for cooperation between the Member States and the Commission regarding FDI that is likely to affect security or public order. However, since the EU Member States have sole responsibility for their national security, they may decide whether or not to screen FDI.[13] The Regulation sets forth a non-exhaustive list of factors that may be taken into account by the Member States and the EU Commission in assessing whether a given FDI is "likely to affect" security or public order.[14]

[8] Cf. e.g. Appellate Body Report, *US – Foreign Sales Corporations* (Recourse to Art.21.5), WT/DS108/AB/RW, adopted 29 January 2002, DSR 2002:I, p. 55, paras 207 ff with further references.

[9] On this see Vranes (2009a).

[10] GATT Panel Report, *Canada – Administration of the Foreign Investment Review Act*, L/5504, adopted 7 February 1984, BISD 30S/140 (hereinafter Panel Report, *Canada – FIRA*).

[11] Panel Report, *European Union and its member States – Certain Measures Relating to the Energy Sector*, WT/DS476/R, circulated to WTO Members 10 August 2018 [appealed by the European Union on 21 September 2018] (hereinafter: Panel Report, *EU – Energy*).

[12] The Report has been appealed by the EU to the EU Appellate Body. Since the Appellate Body has not been functioning since December 2019 (given that the US has been blocking the appointment of new judges for several years), the Report has not become legally binding.

[13] Art. 1(1) through 1(3) of the Screening Regulation.

[14] Art. 4 of the Screening Regulation.

This list in particular comprises critical infrastructure (including energy infrastructure), critical technologies and dual use items (including e.g. energy storage and nuclear technologies), supply of critical inputs and sensitive information.[15] This listing shows that the concept of "security or public order" as defined in the EU Screening Regulation stretches well beyond the traditional concept of "national security". While this is in line with recent trends in many states,[16] there remains the question whether this broad understanding is in line with relevant WTO disciplines.[17] Furthermore, in determining whether a given investment is likely to affect security or public order, account may be taken in particular of "whether the foreign investor is directly or indirectly controlled by the government, including state bodies or armed forces, of a third country, including through ownership structure or significant funding".[18] As has been observed, this clause is obviously directed against incoming FDI from China and Russia.[19]

The aforementioned mechanism for cooperation basically requires Member States to notify the EU Commission and other Member States about FDI screening activities. Where a Member State e.g. considers that an FDI undergoing screening in another Member State is likely to affect its security or public order, it may provide comments to the Member State where the screening is taking place.[20] Additionally, the Commission may issue opinions to a Member State undertaking a screening.[21] If an FDI project is likely to affect projects or programs of Union interest (including e.g. Trans-European Networks for Energy), then the Member State concerned "shall take utmost account" of a Commission opinion and must provide an explanation to the Commission, it it does not follow its opinion. This type of procedure, which is known from other fields of EU law and is usually referred to as a "comply or explain"-mechanism, is commonly regarded as constituting soft law.[22] Overall, the Regulation leaves ample room for Member States that decide to establish or maintain a national screening mechanism as to how such a mechanism is to be designed under national law.[23] In this regard, the Austrian 2020 Act on Investment Screening[24] serves as an example of a national implementing measure that may cause concerns in particular under WTO transparency standards.[25] Thus, an Annex

[15] Art. 4 of the Screening Regulation.

[16] Dimitropoulos (1999), p. 3; Bohnert (2022), pp. 10 ff, 52.

[17] See *infra*, Sect. 4.3.3.4.

[18] Art. 4(2)(a) of the Screening Regulation.

[19] Rajavuori and Huhta (2020), p. 4.

[20] Art. 6-8 of the Screening Regulation.

[21] Art. 6-8 of the Screening Regulation.

[22] As will be explained below, such mechanisms too may be caught by WTO law (see *infra*, Sect. 4.1.3.3).

[23] For a discussion of the example of German law cf. e.g. Herrmann (2019), pp. 43 ff; for the example of the 2020 Austrian Act on Investment Screening cf. Vranes (2023), pp. 17 ff.

[24] Austrian *Bundesgesetz über die Kontrolle von ausländischen Direktinvestitionen (Investitionskontrollgesetz)*, Austrian Federal Gazette BGBl. I Nr 87/2022.

[25] On these standards see below, Sect. 4.1.3.

of the Austrian Act contains two parts, the first of which lists sectors that are regarded as particularly sensitive; this list comprises e.g. critical infrastructure. A second part of the Annex contains an additional list, which refers to critical infrastructure such as energy and energy supply. Hence, there is a risk of overlaps between these lists. Likewise, there are unclarities as regards the thresholds which trigger screening under the Austrian Act.[26]

4.1.3 WTO Disciplines Relevant for Investment Screening

As indicated, the GATT and the GATS set forth the disciplines that are primarily significant for investment screening.[27]

4.1.3.1 Pertinent GATT Obligations

First, according to the national treatment principle of the GATT, imported products must receive treatment no less favourable than "like domestic" products in respect of all national measures "affecting their internal sale, offering for sale, purchase, transportation, distribution or use" (Art. III:4). As had been found already in the aforementioned *FIRA* case, trade-related investment measures like *investment screening* – including screening decisions in individual cases—risk violating Art. III:4, if they potentially modify the competitive opportunities to the detriment of "like" imported products.[28] Whereas divergent approaches had been taken to define the concept of "like products", WTO dispute settlement practice has meanwhile clarified that likeness has to be assessed based on the competitive relationship between the products in question.[29] Furthermore, it must be determined whether the

---

[26] Cf. Vranes (2023), pp. 18–19 with further references.

[27] The relevance of the WTO TRIMs Agreement is quite limited, given that it in principle merely confirms the relevance of Arts. III and XI of the GATT for trade-related investment measures (cf. Vranes (2023), pp. 23–24). Furthermore, the WTO Government Procurement Agreement (which e.g. prohibits that suppliers are accorded less favourable treatment on the basis of foreign affiliation or ownership), the Agreement on Subsidies and Countervailing Measures (which is relevant e.g. in the case of undue incentives) and the TRIPS Agreement (which facilitates foreign investments by protecting intellectual property rights) are relevant for foreign investments. Cf. e.g. Eberhard et al. (2021), p. 88.

[28] Panel Report, *Canada – FIRA*, paras 5.12 and 6.1.

[29] Cf. Pirlot (2017), pp. 208 ff; on these and the following issues cf. also Vranes (2009c), pp. 191 ff with further references. It can be argued, in support of this view, that the context established by Art. III:1 and Art. III:2 second sentence as well as the *telos* of Arts. III:2 and III:4 and the overall object and purpose of WTO law indicate that "likeness' in Art. III should be interpreted against the background of protectionism: "like products' should primarily be understood to mean products that are in a *competitive relation* that is even *closer* than that of DCS products, which are mentioned in Art. III:2 second sentence and the Note ad Art. III.

imported products at issue receive "less favourable treatment". This standard, which had given rise to intense academic discussions in the early years of the WTO, has meanwhile been clarified in WTO jurisprudence, the Appellate Body having summarized relevant case law in the following manner: first, the requirement of not according less favourable treatment to imported products calls for effective equality of competitive opportunities between domestic and like imported products; second, a formal difference in treatment is neither necessary nor sufficient to establish less favourable treatment; third, the implications of a contested measure for the equality of competitive conditions between domestic and like must be assessed; fourth, there has to be a "genuine relationship" between the contested measure and the detrimental impact on competitive conditions for imported products.[30]

Secondly, Art. XI:1 of the GATT lays down a general prohibition on quantitative restrictions and related measures,[31] which is also directly relevant for trade-related *investment* measures.[32] Pursuant to WTO jurisprudence, the scope of Art. XI is comprehensive and extends *beyond quantitative restrictions* in a strict sense, as it applies to *all measures other than* measures taking the form of duties, taxes or other charges;[33] also, it is not necessary that such measures are administered at the border.[34] Moreover, it suffices that such a measure has the effect of limiting the competitive opportunities available to imports.[35] Hence, it has been observed that measures that are "capable of impeding trade, directly or indirectly, actually or potentially" could come within the broad category of quantitative restrictions.[36] Therefore, as has been confirmed in GATT/WTO case law, investment screening measures can also come under the purview of Art. XI.[37]

Thirdly, the most-favoured-nation clause enshrined in Art. I of the GATT (which prohibits discriminatory treatment of like imported products) is of particular significance for *investment screening*, as screening mechanisms often *de jure* or *de facto*

[30] Cf. Appellate Body Report, *European Communities – Seal Products*, WT/DS400/AB/R and WT/DS401/AB/R, adopted 18 June 2014, DSR 2014:I, p. 7, para. 5.101. Furthermore, it has been clarified that additional administrative burdens on imported products may amount to less favourable treatment. On all of this cf. Van den Bossche and Zdouc (2022), pp. 433 ff with further references.

[31] According to Art. XI, "[n]o prohibitions or restrictions other than duties, taxes or other charges, whether made effective through quotas…*or other measures*, shall be instituted or maintained by any contracting party on the importation of any product of the territory of any other contracting party" (emphasis added).

[32] This relevance is also underlined by Art. 2.1 of the TRIMs Agreement, according to which trade-related investment measures must not be inconsistent with Art. XI of the GATT.

[33] Cf. Van den Bossche and Zdouc (2022), p. 525 with further references.

[34] On all of this cf. the Panel Report, *EU – Energy*, para. 7.975 with further references to WTO case law.

[35] Such effects need not be quantified, but can be demonstrated through the design, architecture and revealing structure of the measure at issue" (cf. the Panel Report, *EU – Energy*, para. 7.982 with further references).

[36] Choukroune and Nedumpara (2021), p. 102.

[37] Cf. the Panel Report, *Panel on Japanese Measures on Imports of Leather*, 15 May 1984, L/5623, paras. 47–48, 53, 55.

condition the admission of investors on their country of origin, by e.g. requiring scrutiny as to whether an investor is connected to or controlled by a foreign government.[38]

Fourthly, Art. X of the GATT sets out a series of information, publication and transparency requirements that WTO Members must comply with,[39] which are likewise relevant for investment screening, not least because screening procedures have been described as habitually having a "black box" character, risking to lead to unpredictable outcomes.[40]

4.1.3.2 Pertinent GATS Obligations

The GATS "applies to measures by Members *affecting* trade in services"[41] including *foreign direct investments* ("commercial presence" in GATS terminology; cf Art. I of the GATS). Hence, the GATS is directly relevant for investment screening. As indicated, the notion of "commercial presence" also includes the *pre*-establishment phase. WTO Members can even bring complaints in order to protect potential providers of services (and, by implication, *potential investors*),[42] which is pertinent for investment screening.[43]

The GATS disciplines that are of primary importance for investment screening are those on national treatment (Art. XVII), market access (Art. XVI), most-favoured-nation treatment (Art. II; MFN treatment), transparency (Art. III) and domestic regulation (Art. VI). First, according to Art. XVII, if a WTO Member has undertaken ("scheduled") a commitment in a given services sector and its screening measures affect services or investments in the sense of "commercial presence", then it must be analysed, under Art. XVII, whether the foreign service suppliers in question and their services are accorded "less favourable" treatment[44] than the host coun-

[38] An example is Art. 4(2) of the EU Screening Regulation, which cites the criterion of whether an investor is "directly or indirectly controlled" by foreign governments as a factor relevant for determining whether an investment is likely to affect security or public order. On this see also below, Sect. 4.1.3.

[39] On this and relevant case law cf. Van den Bossche and Zdouc (2022), pp. 544 ff; see also Delimatsis (2007), pp. 13 ff; note that the 2017 Trade Facilitation Agreement contains further details, see Weiss et al. (2022), pp. 183–184, 195 ff.

[40] Cheng (2021), p. 565.

[41] On this cf. also Pitschas (2003), p. 71, paras 6 ff, 27 ff, 89 ff et passim; Pauwelyn (2003), pp. 399 ff; Krajewski (2003), pp. 62–73.

[42] Cf. the WTO Panel Report, *European Communities – Regime for the Importation, Sale and Distribution of Bananas*, Complaint by the United States, WT/DS27/R/USA, adopted 25 September 1997, DSR 1997:II, 943 (EC – Bananas III), paras 7.298 ff.

[43] Cf. Zdouc (1999), pp. 325 ff; Vranes (2003), pp. 98–99.

[44] As respects the sub-test of "less favourable treatment", Art. XVII:3 of the GATS stipulates that directly and indirectly discriminatory treatment ("formally identical" and "formally different" treatment in the terminology of Art. XVII:2 and XVII:3 of the GATS) shall be considered as violating the national treatment obligation if it modifies the conditions of competition in favour of like

try's "own like services and service suppliers".[45] Secondly, Art. XVI:1 of the GATS lays down prohibitions on quantitative limitations for foreign services and service providers. Thirdly, pursuant to the GATS MFN clause, WTO Members must accord "to services and service suppliers of any other Member treatment no less favourable than that it accords to like services and service suppliers of any other country" (Art. II:1 of the GATS). Fourthly, the transparency principle set out in Art. III requires each WTO Member to promptly publish all measures of general application that are relevant for the operation of the GATS agreement. Furthermore, it follows from Art. VI that screening mechanisms must be designed and applied in a reasonable, objective and impartial manner.[46]

The fact that these GATS disciplines are clearly significant for investment screening in general and the *energy* sector in particular is underlined by the *EU – Energy* dispute, in which Russia had challenged several EU measures under these provisions as well.[47]

4.1.3.3 Potential Violations of the GATT and GATS

As indicated, the scope of interaction between EU investment screening and WTO law is considerable due to the fact that the GATT and GATS apply to any measures *affecting* trade in goods, services or investments ("commercial presence"). Since it suffices that a measure has a certain "degree of authoritativeness",[48] even soft law-type measures like the "comply or explain mechanism" that has been built into the EU Screening Regulation may become relevant under WTO law.[49]

Turning to concrete examples, there is a risk that screening decisions that do not authorize investments originating in a given WTO Member could be challenged on

---

domestic services or service suppliers. Additionally, Footnote 10 of the GATS makes it clear that commitments assumed by WTO Members under Art. XVII in their schedules "shall not be construed to require any Member to compensate for any inherent competitive disadvantages which result from the foreign character of the relevant services or service suppliers".

[45] Regarding the issue of "like services" and "like service suppliers", it has been clarified in WTO dispute settlement that these terms have to be treated as an integrated concept that does not require two separate findings. Similarly to the GATT context, it is necessary to determine whether the services and services are in a competitive relationship with each other. If this relationship is close enough, then the foreign and domestic services and service suppliers have to be regarded as being "like" each other. On this cf. Van den Bossche and Zdouc (2022), pp. 445 ff with further references; Weiss et al. (2022), p. 348 with further references. Art. XVII had been applied to investment screening also in the aforementioned Panel Report, *EU – Energy* (at paras 7.1056 ff).

[46] Fassion and Natens (2020), p. 123.

[47] WTO Panel Report, *European Union and its Member States – Certain Measures Relating to the Energy Sector*, WT/DS476/R, circulated to WTO Members 10 August 2018 [appealed by the European Union on 21 September 2018] (in the following: *EU – Energy*), paras 7.1255 ff.

[48] See *Van den Bossche/Zdouc*, pp. 544–545 (citing the Panel Reports, *EC – Information Technology Products*, WT/DS375/R, WT/DS376/R, WT/DS377/R, adopted 21 September 2010, DSR 2010:III, p. 933, para. 7.1027).

[49] Cf. Vranes (2023), p. 28.

the basis of the MFN principles of the GATT and the GATS. A case in point is the aforementioned clause of the EU Screening Regulation, which cites the criterion of whether an investor is "directly or indirectly controlled" by foreign governments as a factor relevant for determining whether an investment is likely to affect security or public order. Similarly, screening decisions taken in individual cases could be challenged by invoking the GATT national treatment clause (which e.g. the US successfully did in the *Canada – FIRA* case[50]) or Arts. XI, XVI and XVII of the GATS (as Russia had tried in the *EU – Energy* case).[51]

Another example that may be problematic from the viewpoint of the GATT and GATS transparency standards are the rules in the Austrian Investment Act implementing the EU Screening Regulation, which, as indicated above, have been regarded as being rather unclear: this in particular includes the Annex of the Austrian Act on Investment Screening with its two parts that list particularly sensitive sectors on the one hand and "other sectors" on the other hand, both parts being subject to different thresholds that trigger investment screening.[52] Since there are overlaps between these lists, which also concern *energy*,[53] it is not sufficiently clear *ex ante* in which cases investments will be subject to screening. Furthermore, the duration of the review of investment screening decisions in the complex EU multilevel system could raise concerns, given that unduly long review proceedings have been found to violate Art. X:3(a) of the GATT.[54] Further examples of violations of relevant GATT and GATS provisions have been discussed in the literature.[55]

4.1.3.4 Justification of Violations of WTO Law

A measure that *prima facie* violates GATT or GATS obligations can still be justified under the so-called "general exception" clauses of the GATT and the GATS (Arts. XX GATT and XIV GATS) and the "security exceptions" in these agreements (Arts. XXI GATT and XIV*bis* GATS).

General Exceptions in the GATT and GATS

Turning to the "general exceptions" first, since the EU Screening Regulation is meant to scrutinize investments that may affect "security or public order",[56] the clauses principally relevant are Arts. XX(d) and XX(j) of the GATT and Art. XIV(a)

---

[50] See above, Sect. 4.1.3.1.

[51] See above, Sects. 4.1.1 and 4.1.3.2.

[52] Cf. above, Sect. 4.1.2.

[53] Cf. above, Sect. 4.1.2.

[54] Cf. Van den Bossche and Zdouc (2022), p. 553 with further references.

[55] Cf. Vranes (2023), pp. 54 ff.

[56] See above, Sect. 4.1.2.

of the GATS. Given that the Screening Regulation explicitly to refers to Art. XIV(a) GATS as well as for space constraints, we will concentrate on this provision in the following (the justification of screening measures under Arts. XX(d) and XX(j) of the GATT has already been discussed elsewhere[57]).

Art. XIV(a) of the GATS makes it possible to justify restrictive measures that are "necessary [...] to maintain public order". In interpreting this provision, regard must be had to Footnote 5, attached to this provision, which underlines that "[t]he public order exception may be invoked only where a genuine and sufficiently serious threat is posed to one of the fundamental interests of society". The central criterion in this clause is "necessary to", which has largely been interpreted, by the Appellate Body, by analogy with the "necessity" test developed under Art. XX of the GATT, [58] as requiring a process of "weighing and balancing" taking into account in particular a measure's contribution to a legitimate policy goal, the importance of this goal, and the degree of a measure's trade effect.[59]

It is of particular relevance for the *energy context* that in applying this "weighing and balancing" analysis, the panel in *EU – Energy* found that *energy security* is of fundamental importance. It then inquired into whether the screening mechanism at issue was manifestly apt to contribute to the maintenance of public order and whether the degree of trade-restrictiveness of this screening measure was not undue. This thus amounts to a case-by-case approach the outcome of which is difficult to predict (this test was found to be fulfilled *in casu*, given that the prohibition on investments only applied in cases of threat to energy security).[60]

Importantly, it is not sufficient that an investment screening activity is found to comply with Art. XIV(a), given that it must additionally be shown that measures found to be provisionally justified under this provision are also consistent with the introductory paragraph of Art. XIV, the so-called Chapeau. In the *EU – Energy* case, the panel took a distinctly restrictive approach to this clause. While the panel acknowledged that foreign controlled investors may be influenced by foreign governments, it argued that this reasoning may apply to domestically controlled investors, too. While it in fact conceded that this threat of undue foreign influence for the EU's energy security may be higher as regards persons controlled by foreign

---

[57] Vranes (2023), pp. 57 ff.

[58] Appellate Body Report, *United States – Measures Affecting the Cross-Border Supply of Gambling and Betting Services*, WT/DS285/AB/R, adopted 20 April 2005, DSR 2005:XII, p. 5663 (*US – Gambling*), paras 306 ff; on the necessity test under Art. XX of the GATT, see also below, Sect. 4.2.3.5.1.

[59] Appellate Body Report, *Korea – Measures Affecting Imports of Fresh, Chilled and Frozen Beef*, WT/DS161/AB/R, WT/DS169/AB/R, adopted 10 January 2001, DSR 2001:I, p. 5 (hereinafter *Korea – Beef*), para. 164. In the words of the Appellate Body: "[t]he more vital or important [the goals pursued] are, the easier it would be to accept as "necessary' a measure designed as an enforcement instrument" (para. 162); "[t]he greater the contribution [of a measure to the goal pursued], the more easily a measure might be considered to be "necessary'" (para. 163; moreover, "[a] measure with a relatively slight impact upon imported products might more easily be considered as "necessary' than a measure with intense or broader restrictive effects" (para. 163).

[60] Panel Report, *EU – Energy*, paras 7.1209 ff.

governments,[61] it took issue with the fact that the EU had not addressed the threat posed by foreign governments requiring or inducing domestically controlled suppliers of *energy services* to undermine the security of the EU's energy supply as well. Having applied this consistency test, the panel concluded that the EU's measure constituted "arbitrary and unjustifiable discrimination" violating the Chapeau.[62] If this quite exacting approach were applied to the EU Screening Regulation, then this could have problematic consequences: On the one hand, the Regulation requires the Member States to adopt measures to prevent circumventions of their screening mechanisms;[63] on the other hand, neither the Regulation nor the example of the Austrian Act contain clear guidance in this respect.

Security Exceptions in the GATT and GATS

Since the EU Screening Regulation—like most investment screening mechanisms—is also aimed at protecting national security (besides public order), the security exceptions in the GATT (Art. XXI) and GATS (Art. XIV*bis*) are of key significance for the *energy security* context as well. These provisions essentially make it possible for WTO Members to justify trade-restrictive measures which they consider necessary for the protection of their essential security interests.[64]

The functioning of the security exception of the GATT (and the analogous security exception in the TRIPS Agreement) has been clarified in a series of recent high-profile trade disputes.[65] These reports are clearly also relevant regarding the textually

---

[61] Panel Report, *EU – Energy*, para. 7.1250.

[62] Panel Report, *EU – Energy*, para. 7.1253.

[63] Art. 3(1) of the Regulation.

[64] Art. XXI of the GATT provides in relevant part that

> [n]othing in this Agreement shall be construed

(a) to require any contracting party to furnish any information the disclosure of which it considers contrary to its essential security interests; or
(b) to prevent any contracting party from taking any action which it considers necessary for the protection of its essential security interests

(i) relating to fissionable materials or the materials from which they are derived;
(ii) relating to the traffic in arms, ammunition and implements of war and to such traffic in other goods and materials as is carried on directly or indirectly for the purpose of supplying a military establishment;
(iii) taken in time of war or other emergency in international relations.

[65] Panel Report, *Russia – Traffic in Transit*, WT/DS512/R, adopted 26 April 2019, DSR 2019:VIII, p. 4301; cf. also the so-called US – Steel proceedings triggered by China, Norway, Switzerland and Turkey (*United States – Certain Measures on Steel and Aluminium Products*, WT/DS544/R, Add.1 and Suppl.1, circulated to WTO Members 9 December 2022 (*US – Steel (China)), United States – Certain Measures on Steel and Aluminium Products*, WT/DS552/R, Add.1 and Suppl.1, circulated to WTO Members 9 December 2022 (*US – Steel (Norway), United States – Certain Measures on*

and structurally almost identical security exception of the GATS (Art. XIV*bis*), which has not yet been invoked in WTO proceedings, but has explicitly been regarded as a provision that is "equivalent" to Art. XXI of the GATT.[66]

As a matter of considerable systemic importance, the panel reports in these disputes have clarified that the security exceptions are justiciable, which means that the mere invocation of these provisions does not automatically oust a panel's jurisdiction.[67] Furthermore, contrary to views held by some WTO Members and academics, it has been found that these exceptions are not subject to the unilateral discretionary interpretation by the Member invoking them, but are amenable to objective determination.[68] Moreover, the panel in the seminal *Russia – Traffic* case has clarified the pivotal concept "emergency in international relations" in Art. XXI(b)(iii) (to be found also in Art. XIV*bis* of the GATS), submitting that this term encompasses not only defence and military interests, but also "maintenance of law and public order interests".[69] Crucially, the panel in *Russia – Traffic* applied a very low standard of review in general and under this provision's introductory paragraph (Chapeau) in particular, according to which a WTO Member may take "any action *which it considers necessary for* the protection of its *essential security interests*". This wording was regarded, by the panel, as not giving *carte blanche* to WTO Members, but as being confined by the principle of good faith; hence, WTO Members must not circumvent their GATT obligations by simply "re-labelling trade interests" as essential security interests.[70] A WTO Member invoking this provision must therefore articulate these interests "sufficiently enough to demonstrate their veracity".[71] Adopting a "sliding scale" approach,[72] the panel furthermore stressed that the further an "emergency in international relations", which is invoked by a WTO Member, appears

Steel and Aluminium Products, WT/DS556/R, Add.1 and Suppl.1, circulated to WTO Members 9 December 2022 (*US – Steel (Switzerland)), United States – Certain Measures on Steel and Aluminium Products*, WT/DS564/R, Add.1 and Suppl.1, circulated to WTO Members 9 December 2022 (*US – Steel (Turkey)*); Panel Report, *Saudi Arabia – Measures Concerning the Protection of Intellectual Property Rights*, WT/DS567/R and Add.1, circulated to WTO Members on 16 June 2020; Panel Report, *US – Origin Marking Requirement*, WT/DS597/R, circulated to Members 21 December 2022.

[66] Panel Report, *Russia—Traffic in Transit*, para. 7.20; on this and the following cf. Vranes (2023), pp. 44 ff with further references to pertinent panel reports.

[67] Panel Report, *Russia – Traffic in Transit*, paras 7.53-7.56, 7.79 and 7.83-7.100; see also Panel Report, *Saudi Arabia – IPRs*, paras 7.7-7.23; Panel Report, *US – Steel (China)*, paras 7.122 - 7.128; Panel Report, *US – Origin Marking Requirement*, paras 7.42-7.190.

[68] Panel report, *Russia – Traffic in Transit*, paras 7.69 ff. These findings are in line with several views expressed in the academic literature; cf. in particular Schill and Briese (2009), pp. 96 ff, 106 ff.

[69] Panel report, *Russia – Traffic in Transit*, para 7.74.

[70] Panel Report, *Russia – Traffic in Transit*, para. 7.133.

[71] Panel Report, *Russia – Traffic in Transit*, para. 7.134.

[72] Van den Bossche and Zdouc (2022), fn 162 with further references.

removed from an armed conflict, the greater the specificity would be required in the argumentation of the WTO Member concerned.[73]

These elucidations are specifically significant for the *energy* context and the example of the EU Screening Regulation, given that the Regulation refers to sectors and projects where *energy and security dimensions* are closely interwoven, such as dual use items (including e.g. nuclear technologies, energy storage) and the Trans-European Networks for Energy, Transport and Telecommunications and other projects;[74] similarly, the Austrian Act e.g. refers to energy, critical infrastructure, artificial intelligence and energy supply as areas of concern.[75] In view of this case law, EU Member States would arguably be in a position to justify in particular screening measures "taken in time of war or emergency in international relations", if, firstly, such a crisis can be objectively determined and if the state, secondly, can show that the screening activities are not implausible as measures protecting essential security interests. The latter, thirdly, would have to be articulated with sufficient clarity, taking into account the aforementioned sliding-scale approach, according to which the burden of argumentation varies in relation to the extent that an emergency in international relations appears (more or less) removed from an armed conflict.[76]

4.2 The EU's CBAM Device and WTO Law

The second horizontal instrument that is regarded as being necessary to protect the EU's Internal Energy Market is the EU's Carbon Border Adjustment Mechanism (CBAM). This Chapter briefly explains the relevance of carbon border adjustment for the EU energy sector (Sect. 4.2.1), before it outlines the EU CBAM Regulation (Sect. 4.2.2). It then examines to what extent this regulation risks violating fundamental WTO disciplines and whether any prima facie violations of WTO rules could be justified under the general exceptions of the WTO GATT Agreement (Sect. 4.1.3).

4.2.1 Carbon Border Adjustment and the Energy Sector

As explained above, the Internal Energy Market (IEM) is meant to contribute to the EU's goal of strategic energy autonomy (SEA). This requires instruments preventing the risk that EU undertakings relocate to third countries.[77] The EU's long-

[73] Panel Report, *Russia – Traffic in Transit*, para 7.135 (italics added). On the divergent approach of the panel in *Saudi Arabia – IPRs* see in the following text.

[74] Cf. above, Sect. 4.1.2.

[75] Cf. above, Sect. 4.1.2.

[76] Cf. Vranes (2023), pp. 42 ff and 60–61 for further details.

[77] Cf. above, Chaps. 2 and 3.

awaited Carbon Border Adjustment Mechanism (CBAM) has been enacted in order to mitigate this risk. In the energy context, the relevance of the CBAM is underlined by the fact that it covers energy products, goods requiring particularly energy-intensive production methods as well as products regarded as crucial inputs in the EU's envisaged transition to green energy.[78]

The CBAM was enacted in May 2023 and has been in force since October 2023.[79] Other options, which had been explored by the EU Commission, such as the introduction of a new carbon customs duty or a carbon tax on selected products, have not been further pursued.[80] The CBAM is part of the European Green Deal (EGD), which aims at transforming the EU into an economy without net emissions by 2050.[81] This effort must be seen against the backdrop of the 2015 Paris Agreement,[82] under which the parties have committed to hold the increase in the global average temperature well below 2 °C above pre-industrial levels and to attempt to limit the increase to 1.5 °C above pre-industrial levels. The EU has undertaken the obligation to reduce its greenhouse gas (GHG) emissions by at least 55% compared to 1990s levels by 2030. These commitments are binding both under international law (within the UNFCCC framework) and EU law.[83] The EU has been striving to comply with these commitments through a series of measures, a central one being the EU Emissions Trading System (ETS).[84] However, the EU is concerned that its ambitious climate policies may increase the threat of "carbon leakage", i.e. the twofold risk of (i) EU producers relocating to third countries with looser environmental policies and (ii) increasing imports into the EU of goods produced abroad with higher GHG emissions.[85]

The EU has therefore decided to introduce the CBAM as a measure complementing the ETS. On the one hand, the CBAM is meant to help the EU achieve its climate protections targets. On the other hand, and this is where international economic law comes into play, it is also "expected to [...] contribute to decarbonization in

[78] Cf. below, Sect. 4.2.2.

[79] Regulation (EU) 2023/956 of the European Parliament and of the Council of 10 May 2023 establishing a carbon border adjustment mechanism. OJ L 130, 16.5.2023, pp. 52–104 (in the following: "CBAM Regulation").

[80] Cf. e.g. Englisch and Falcao (2021), pp. 10857–10858.

[81] On this an the following the CBAM Regulation, Recitals 1 ff; on the background of CBAM see also Englisch and Falcao (2021), pp. 10857 ff; Espa, Francois and van Asselt (2022), pp. 3 ff; Hollaus and Mayr (2022), pp. 102 ff; Quick (2020), pp. 550 ff; Raza et al. (2022), pp. 1 ff.

[82] Cf. the Annex of Decision 1/CP.21 of the Conference of the Parties to the United Nations Framework on Climate Change, FCCC/CP/2015/10/Add.1 ("Paris Agreement"), https://unfccc.int/sites/default/files/resource/docs/2015/cop21/eng/10a01.pdf?download.

[83] Cf. Regulation (EU) 2021/1119 of the European Parliament and of the Council of 30 June 2021 establishing the framework for achieving climate neutrality and amending Regulations (EC) No 401/2009 and (EU) 2018/1999 ("European Climate Law"), OJ L 243, 9.7.2021, pp. 1–17.

[84] Directive 2003/87/EC of the European Parliament and of the Council of 13 October 2003 establishing a scheme for greenhouse gas emission allowance trading within the Community and amending Council Directive 96/61/EC, OJ L 275, 25.10.2003, pp. 32–46.

[85] CBAM Regulation, Recital 18.

third countries", as explicitly underlined by the CBAM Regulation itself,[86] the lever consisting in the economic effects that the CBAM is likely to exert on third countries.[87] Moreover, the CBAM should gradually replace two existing measures that had been instituted so as to mitigate the risk of carbon leakage, namely the free allocation of EU ETS allowances (i.e. tradable emission permits) in economic sectors prone to relocation of production, on the one hand, and financial compensation for indirect emission costs incurred from GHG emission costs that are passed on in electricity prices, on the other hand.[88] The details as to how the phasing out of these measures and the phasing in of the CBAM are to be coordinated have not been enacted so far.[89]

The EU is keen on presenting the CBAM as "a climate measure" that is compatible with WTO law,[90] emphasizing that both the EU ETS and the CBAM "have a *regulatory* nature" (as opposed to a fiscal one),[91] a characterization which, if correct also from the angle of WTO law, is particularly important for the complex question as to how to categorize the CBAM under the GATT.[92]

4.2.2 The CBAM Regulation Outlined

The CBAM requires importers of certain products to surrender CBAM certificates in order to prevent the risk of carbon leakage.[93] These products are listed in Annex I of the Regulation, which comprises electricity, cement, fertilizers, iron and steel, aluminium and chemicals. It thus covers *energy products* (electricity), goods requiring particularly *energy-intensive production methods* (cement, iron and steel, aluminium) as well as products needed as crucial inputs in the EU's envisaged transition to *green energy* (aluminium). Whereas the CBAM applies to these goods when they are imported from third countries, it does not apply to goods originating in third countries to which the EU ETS applies or which have concluded an agreement with the EU fully linking their national emissions trading systems with the EU ETS. So far, the latter derogation covers the Member States of the European Economic Area (EEA) and Switzerland.[94]

---

[86] CBAM Regulation, Recital 10.

[87] See below, Sects. 4.2.2 and 4.2.3.5.6.

[88] CBAM Regulation, Recitals 11 ff.

[89] Cf. Art. 31(2) of the CBAM Regulation, which empowers the Commission to enact these rules in implementing acts.

[90] CBAM Regulation, Recital 15.

[91] CBAM Regulation, Recital 20.

[92] See below, Sect. 4.2.3.3.

[93] Art. 1 of the CBAM Regulation.

[94] Cf. Art. 2(4) ff and Annex III point 1 of the CBAM Regulation. A second derogation of this type theoretically applies to countries or territories that have an electricity market which is integrated

Goods may be imported only by an authorized "CBAM declarant".[95] CBAM declarants are required to submit annual CBAM declarations containing information in particular on the emissions embedded in the goods imported and the corresponding number of CBAM certificates to be surrendered. The importation of goods by other persons is prohibited.[96] Importantly, it is possible to reduce the number of certificates on the account of the carbon price already effectively paid in the country of origin.[97]

Embedded emissions must be determined based on the actual emissions in accordance with the methodology set out in the CBAM Regulation.[98] Where the actual emissions cannot be adequately determined, default values may be used for the determination of embodied emissions.[99] On the other hand, emissions embedded in imported electricity shall be assessed by reference to default values, unless the authorised declarant is able to demonstrate that the criteria to determine the embedded emissions based on the actual emissions listed are met.[100] The CBAM certificates are sold by the EU Member States on a common central platform. Their price is to be calculated as the average of the *weekly prices* of EU ETS allowances.[101] There is no limit on the *number* of CBAM certificates that can be issued;[102] however, they cannot be traded.[103]

4.2.3 WTO Disciplines Relevant for Carbon Border Adjustment

Several WTO Members[104] and academics[105] have claimed that the CBAM violates basic WTO rules. We will examine this issue in this Section.

In assessing the consistency of the CBAM with WTO law, a series of complex legal issues arise under the GATT. A pivotal threshold question is the determination as to whether the CBAM is to be classified as a regulatory or a fiscal measure in

---

with the EU IEM. So far, there are no countries listed under this second derogation (cf. Art. 2(7)-(8) and Annex III point 2 of the CBAM Regulation).

[95] On this concept see in the following.

[96] Art. 25(1) of the CBAM Regulation.

[97] Arts. 6 and 9 of the CBAM Regulation.

[98] Art. 7(2) and points 2 and 3 of Annex IV of the CBAM Regulation.

[99] Art. 7(2) and point 4.1 of Annex IV of the CBAM Regulation.

[100] Art. 7(3) and points 4.2 and 5 of Annex IV of the CBAM Regulation.

[101] Arts. 20 and 21 of the CBAM Regulation.

[102] See also Recital 21 of the CBAM Regulation.

[103] Art. 24 and Recital 24 of the CBAM Regulation.

[104] Cf. WTO Committee on Market Access, Minutes of 16 and 17 October 2023, WTO document G/MA/M/79 of 5 February 2024, pp. 38 ff; see also Erixon (2022) p. 47.

[105] See the various authors cited in the next Section.

terms of the GATT. Depending on this categorization, different rules under the GATT become applicable, which determine the legislative leeway left to the EU.

This Section therefore proceeds as follows: It will first outline the interplay between the GATT disciplines relevant for regulatory measures (*infra*, Sect. 4.2.3.1); it will then sketch out the relationship between the GATT principles that are relevant for national fiscal measures (*infra*, Sect. 4.2.3.2).[106] It will next address the question as to how to classify the CBAM under these two sets of rules (*infra*, Sect. 4.2.3.3). In the light of this classification, it will deal with the issue as to whether the CBAM complies with the relevant substantive GATT rules (*infra*, Sect. 4.2.3.4). Finally, the possibility of justifying potential violations of these GATT disciplines under Art. XX of the GATT will be examined (*infra*, Sect. 4.2.3.5).

4.2.3.1 GATT Non-Discrimination and Market Access Rules Relevant for Regulatory Measures

Determining the GATT's impact on the leeway left to WTO Members with respect to regulatory (as opposed to fiscal) measures in particular requires a legal analysis of a "triangular relationship" in the GATT agreement.[107] This triangle consists of Art. XI (General Elimination of Quantitative Restrictions) dealing with border measures, Art. III:4 (National Treatment) addressing internal regulatory measures and Art. XX (General Exceptions).

In expressing the "tariffs only" principle, which underlies the GATT, Art. XI:1 interdicts all prohibitions or restrictions on importation "other than duties, taxes or other charges".[108] Whether a measure falls to be reviewed under Art. III:4 or Art. XI has considerable consequences for national regulatory autonomy, since Art. XI (just as Art. II[109]) sets forth a *per se* prohibition, which applies subject to justification in particular under Art. XX,[110] whereas measures coming under Art. III:4 are not prohibited *per se*, but only if they are found to be discriminatory.[111]

---

[106] While the focus in the following thus will be on the GATT, relevant rules with similar contents are discussed in Holzer et al. (2022), pp. 31 ff.

[107] This section and the following are based on Vranes, *Trade and the Environment. Fundamental Issues in International and WTO Law* (habilitation thesis, manuscript submitted at Vienna University of Economics and Business (Wirtschaftsuniversitaet Wien)) 2006, 315–319; they have been updated in 2025, taking into account relevant WTO dispute settlement reports and academic writings.

[108] On this principle and the "regulatory philosophy" of the GATT more generally cf. e.g. Trebilcock and Howse (1999), pp. 25 ff, 112 ff; Jackson (1997), pp. 139 ff; and Petersmann (1997), pp. 10 ff.

[109] See below, Sect. 4.2.3.2.

[110] Art. XI forms part of a nuanced rule–exception regime, which is laid down in Arts. XI-XIV. Arts. XI:2 and XII set forth exceptions to the prohibition contained in Art. XI:1. When restrictions are exceptionally permitted, they must, as a rule, be applied on a non-discriminatory basis; there are, however, exceptions also to the latter principle which are laid down in Art. XIV. On this cf. e.g. Sebastian Puth (2003), p. 277; Matsushita et al. (2006), pp. 272 ff.

[111] Cf. Puth (2003), pp. 234–236; Pauwelyn (2005), p. 134; Trüeb (2001), pp. 115 ff.

The reason for the quite different approaches taken in Arts. III:4 and XI can be seen in the economic consideration that measures in the sense of Art. XI are inherently discriminatory and protectionist;[112] as quantitative restrictions, they constitute "strict caps" which cannot be overcome through efforts by the producer.[113] Internal regulations (i.e. measures that typically apply to domestic *and* imported products), on the other hand, are not necessarily protectionist and discriminatory. They may e.g. stipulate qualitative minimum requirements as a precondition for market access, which can be overcome by foreign producers, as opposed to the strict cap effect of quantitative restrictions on importation.[114]

The GATT explicitly addresses this issue in the Note ad Art. III, pursuant to which:

> Any internal tax or other internal charge, or any law, regulation or requirement of the kind referred to in paragraph 1 which *applies* to an imported product *and* to the like domestic product and is collected or enforced in the case of the imported product at the time or point of importation, is nevertheless to be regarded as an internal tax or other internal charge, or a law, regulation or requirement of the kind referred to in paragraph 1, and *is accordingly subject to the provisions of Art. III.*[115]

Hence, the aforesaid economic consideration is reflected in the Note ad Art. III, which carves out any measures from the scope of Art. XI, which are enforced at the border and which therefore might appear to fall under this provision, whenever such measures actually apply both to domestic and foreign products. In this logic, the details of such measures have to be scrutinized under Art. III:4, in order to ascertain whether they are discriminatory.

This approach is reflected in GATT/WTO jurisprudence, where in *EC – Asbestos*, for example, the French measure banning the importation of asbestos was examined under Art. III:4, given that the ban applied also to domestic products.[116] Essentially the same attitude has been taken in dispute settlement practice under the GATT 1947, where panels had held that Art. XI regulates "measures affecting the 'importation' of products", whereas Art. III was characterized as dealing with measures "affecting 'imported products'".[117] Still, it must be pointed out that the term "affecting", which is not used in the Note ad Art. III, is ambiguous, given that any internal

---

[112] Cf. also Winter (2001), pp. 71, 79 ff; Pauwelyn (2005), pp. 134 ff.

[113] Weiler (2000), pp. 201 ff; Pauwelyn (2005), pp. 134 ff; Matsushita et al. (2006), pp. 269 ff.

[114] Cf. Weiler (2000), pp. 201 ff; Pauwelyn (2005), pp. 134 ff; this difference is also emphasized, in the context of the GATS, by the 1993 Scheduling Guidelines, GATT DOC MTN.GNS/W/164 of 3 September 1993, para 5; with respect to the similar issue under the GATS cf. Delimatsis (2006), p. 1070.

[115] Emphasis added.

[116] Panel Report, *European Communities – Measures Affecting Asbestos and Asbestos-Containing Products*, WT/DS135/R and Add.1, adopted 5 April 2001, as modified by Appellate Body Report WT/DS135/AB/R, DSR 2001:VIII, p. 3305 (in the following: *EC – Asbestos*), para 8.93; see also the Panel Report, *India – Measures Affecting the Automotive Sector*, WT/DS146/R, WT/DS175/R, and Corr.1, adopted 5 April 2002, DSR 2002:V, p. 1827, paras 7.259–7.261.

[117] Panel report, *Canada – FIRA*, para 5.14; concurring, panel report, *US – Measures Affecting Alcoholic and Malt Beverages*, adopted on 19 June 1992, DS23/R - 39S/206 (*US – Malt*), para 5.63.

regulations, which are addressed under Art. III, may *also* have effects on importation, even if they are non-discriminatory in law and fact. If this were overlooked and any measures affecting importation were scrutinized under Art. XI, the GATT would risk being transformed from a non-discrimination regime into a market access regime. By contrast, the logic of the Note ad Art. III, and the underlying economic rationale, clearly suggest that a regulatory measure, which is applicable to both domestic and imported products, has to be examined under Art. III:4, even if such a measure *affects* importation. In this regard, it is immaterial that an internal measure is enforced vis à vis foreign and domestic products through different means (ie through trade measures at the border and other internal enforcement measures);[118] it is pivotal, by contrast, that the regulation of imported and domestic products is *equivalent*.[119]

Hence, a "border adjustment" of internal regulatory measures is possible, in principle. This is of particular relevance for the CBAM, if the latter is regarded as having regulatory character.[120]

4.2.3.2 GATT Non-Discrimination and Market Access Rules Relevant for Fiscal Measures

A second "triangular" relationship, which is similar to the relationship between Art. III:4, XI and XX, exists with respect to national *fiscal* measures. It results from the interplay between Art. II, which addresses border measures (customs duties and all other duties and charges "imposed on or in connection with importation"), Art. III:2, which deals with internal taxation, and Art. XX. The problem is that taxes and charges which are levied on domestic products are often imposed on foreign products *on importation*. This raises the question as to whether such measures are to be regarded as internal taxes or charges, which are subject to a test of discrimination under Art. III:2, or as border measures, which fall under the prohibition set forth in Art. II:1(b). In this context, the Note ad Art. III steps in again, attempting to clarify the relationship between Art. II:1(b) and Art. III:2. As mentioned before, according to this Note, "[a]ny internal tax or other internal charge [...] which applies to an imported product *and* to the like domestic product and is collected [...] in the case of the imported product at the time or point of importation, is nevertheless to be regarded as an internal tax or other internal charge [...] and *is accordingly subject to the provisions of Art. III*."

Importantly for present purposes, it is the interplay between these provisions which makes a border adjustment of taxes (BTA) possible.[121] BTAs are a classic

[118] Cf. the panel report, *US – Section 337 of the Tariff Act of 1930*, adopted on 7 November 1989, L/6439 - 36S/345 (*US – Section 337*), para 5.11.

[119] Cf. also Puth (2003), p. 236.

[120] On the consequences of such classification cf infra, Sect. 4.2.3.4.

[121] On this and the following see also Vranes (2016), pp. 77 ff; Vranes (2021), pp. 189 ff.

instrument of trade policy that has been used for many decades, in particular in relation to value added taxes.[122] According to a definition provided by the 1970 GATT Working Party on Border Tax Adjustment, which is based on Guidelines of the Organisation for Economic Co-operation and Development (OECD), BTAs are:

> any fiscal measures which [...] enable exported products to be relieved of some or all of the tax charged in the exporting country in respect of similar domestic products sold to consumers on the home market and which enable imported products sold to consumers to be charged with some or all of the tax charged in the importing country in respect of similar domestic products.[123]

While taxes constitute instruments that may be environmentally and economically preferable to command-and-control-type regulation in certain constellations,[124] they will regularly evoke competitiveness concerns.[125] It is for the latter reason that GATT/WTO law has provided for rules on BTA, according to which a Member may impose an adjusting tax on importation that is equivalent to a comparable internal tax levied on like domestic products. Likewise, on the export side, a country is authorized to exempt products to be exported from taxes borne by like products that are destined for domestic consumption.[126] Excessive adjustment on the import or export side is deemed to constitute a violation of national treatment or an export subsidy, respectively.[127] Contrary to what the notion "border tax adjustment" may imply, such adjustment does not necessarily take place at the border, notably since imported goods, like domestic products, may be taxed at the time when they are sold.[128]

Relevant WTO rules are laid down in the GATT and the WTO Agreement on Subsidies and Countervailing Measures (ASCM). On the import side, these comprise the aforementioned provisions of Art. III:2, Art. II:2(a) and the Note ad Art. III of the GATT; on the export side, pertinent obligations are set forth in Art. XVI, the Note ad Art. XVI, Arts. VI:4 and VII:3 of the GATT, the footnote 1 to Art. 1.1(ii) of the ASCM Agreement, Annex I paras (g) and (h), Annex II and footnote 61 of the ASCM Agreement.[129]

Underlying these provisions is the distinction between *direct taxes*, which are imposed on the producer, and *indirect taxes*, which are applied, directly or

---

[122] Holzer (2010), pp. 51 ff; Ruddigkeit (2009), p. 5.

[123] Cf. the report of the 1970 GATT Working Party on Border Tax Adjustment, GATT Doc L/3464, 20 November 1970. Available at: https://docs.wto.org/gattdocs/q/GG/L3799/3464.PDF).

[124] Cf. e.g. Committee on Trade and Environment, Taxes and Charges for Environmental Purposes. Border Tax Adjustment. Note by the Secretariat, WTO Doc WT/CTE/W/47, 2 May 1997, paras 3 ff, 16 ff; Trüeb (2001), pp. 127 ff.

[125] Cottier and Shariff (2013), p. 435; Hillman (2013), p. 1 ff; O'Brien (2009), p. 1094; Pauwelyn (2012), pp. 1 ff.

[126] Cf. e.g. Jackson (1997), pp. 218–219; Puth (2003), pp. 260 ff.

[127] Cf. in the following text.

[128] This is pointed out by the report of the Working Party on Border Tax Adjustment, L/3464, 20 November 1970, para 5. Available at: http://gatt.stanford.edu/page/home.

[129] For a discussion of these rules cf. in the following text.

indirectly, to products. Only indirect taxes can be adjusted under the GATT, as has repeatedly been emphasized in Working Party reports[130] and GATT/WTO dispute settlement.[131] This distinction has its basis in the economic assumption that direct taxes are "shifted backward" so that they are paid by the producer of a good, whereas indirect taxes are considered to be fully "shifted forward" into the price of the final product. Thereby, WTO law incorporates the origin principle for direct taxes and the destination principle for indirect taxes.[132] As these principles are meant to ensure trade neutrality, a product theoretically moves on a level playing field.[133] The underlying economic assumptions on backward and forward shifting of direct and indirect taxes have meanwhile been called into question, however.[134] Thus, the distinction in WTO law has arguably been maintained for pragmatic reasons, in particular for the fact that direct taxes are considered as generally incurring a greater risk of protectionist over-adjustment.[135]

With respect to indirect taxes, the question emerges as to which indirect taxes are eligible for adjustment under WTO law. This question concerns the borderline between Arts. II:1(b) and III:2 of the GATT. Whereas Art. II:1(b) *prohibits* the levying of ordinary customs duties in excess of those set out in GATT tariff schedules and also of all other "duties and charges of any kind imposed on or in connection with importation in excess of those imposed on the date of this Agreement", Art. II:2(a) *authorizes* the imposition "at any time on the importation of any product [of] a charge equivalent to an internal tax imposed consistently with the provisions of paragraph 2 of Art. III in respect of the like domestic product or in respect of an article from which the imported product has been manufactured or produced in whole or in part". The different approach taken in Arts. II and III can again be seen as an expression of the aforementioned GATT policy of subjecting unilateral border measures to stricter disciplines than domestic measures (under Art. III).[136]

This makes it pivotal to distinguish between "duties and charges" in the sense of Art. II:1(b), which are prohibited in principle, and "charges" in the sense of Arts. II:2(a) and III:2, which are merely subject to a test of discrimination. This preliminary question is addressed by Art. II:2(a) and the Note ad Art. III, which refer the

---

[130] Cf. the report of the 1960 Working Party on Art. XVI:4, BISD 9S/185, para 5; and the Working Party on Border Tax Adjustment, L/3464, 20 November 1970, para 14.

[131] For an overview cf. Demaret and Stewardson (1994), pp. 8 ff; see also the FSC/ETI case, discussed in Daly (2005), pp. 25; Hillman (2013), p. 5 ff; Pauwelyn (2012), pp. 24 ff.

[132] Cf. Committee on Trade and Environment, Taxes and Charges for Environmental Purposes. Border Tax Adjustment. Note by the Secretariat, WTO Doc WT/CTE/W/47, 2 May 1997, para 35ff; Puth (2003), pp. 262 ff; Demaret and Stewardson (1994), pp. 5 ff; van Calster (2000), p. 418.

[133] Demaret and Stewardson (1994), pp. 5 ff; Working Party on Border Tax Adjustment, L/3464, 20 November 1970, para 9; Jackson (1997), pp. 218; Trüeb (2001), pp. 465 ff.

[134] Cf. the Working Party on Border Tax Adjustment, L/3464, 20 November 1970, para 8 ff; see also Committee on Trade and Environment, Taxes and Charges for Environmental Purposes. Border Tax Adjustment. Note by the Secretariat, WTO Doc WT/CTE/W/47, 2 May 1997, paras 37 ff; Kendall (2012), pp. 64 ff; Low et al. (2012), p. 499.

[135] Demaret and Stewardson (1994), pp. 14–16; Jackson (1997), p. 221.

[136] For a discussion of this GATT philosophy see Vranes (2009b), pp. 953 ff.

scrutiny of taxes imposed on an imported product to the disciplines of Art. III:2, if it is related, in a sufficient degree, to equivalent charges collected internally on like domestic products.[137] This issue has been addressed by the WTO Appellate Body in the *China–Automobile Parts* case, where it held that the distinction between these provisions hinges upon the factor that triggers the obligation to pay the charge: if it "accrues because of an *internal factor* (e.g., because the product was re-sold internally or because the product was used internally)", then it comes under Art. III.[138] However, if the obligation to pay arises *by virtue of importation*, then it has to be assessed under Art. II.[139] In a comparative law perspective, this approach of the Appellate Body arguably was to be expected, when one compares Arts. II and III of the GATT with the analogous provisions in the Treaty on the Functioning of the EU (TFEU) and standing jurisprudence of the European Court of Justice (ECJ).[140]

Importantly, the CBAM relates to the manner in which imported products have been produced. However, it has meanwhile been clarified in WTO dispute settlement practice and academic writings that measures which are applied to products on the basis of their process and production measures do not per se violate GATT disciplines, even if such process and production methods ("ppm") are not physically ascertainable in the products at issue (so called "non-product-related ppm" or "npr ppm" for short).[141]

4.2.3.3 The Legal Nature of CBAM: Regulatory or Fiscal; Internal or Border Measure?

In the light of the above considerations, four questions arise with respect to the classification of the CBAM under the GATT:

1. Should the CBAM be classified as a *fiscal border* measure in the sense of Art. II:1(b), which sets forth strict upper limits for customs duties and "all other duties or charges of any kind imposed on or in connection with importation"?
2. Should the CBAM be categorized as (part of) a *domestic tax scheme* that is applied at the border and falls to be assessed, under Art. III:2, as to whether it is discriminatory in the sense of this provision?

[137] For a detailed discussion see Vranes (2009b), pp. 953 ff.

[138] WTO Appellate Body Reports, *China – Measures Affecting Imports of Automobile Parts*, WT/DS339/AB/R / WT/DS340/AB/R / WT/DS342/AB/R, adopted 12 January 2009, DSR 2009:I, p. 3 (in the following: *China–Automobile Parts*), para 163.

[139] WTO Appellate Body, *China–Automobile Parts*, paras 159 ff; see also Hillman (2013), p. 5, note 12; Low et al. (2012), pp. 488 ff; Pauwelyn (2012), p. 24.

[140] Cf. Vranes (2009b), pp. 953 ff.

[141] On this see below, Sect. 4.2.3.4.2.

3. Should the CBAM be regarded as a *regulatory border* measure in terms of Art. XI, the scope of which is comprehensive and extends *beyond quantitative restrictions* in a strict sense?[142]
4. Should the CBAM be classified as (part of) a *domestic regulatory* scheme that is applied at the border and needs to be assessed, under Art. III:4, as to whether it is discriminatory in the sense of this provision?

As has been explained above, the categorization of the CBAM as a (fiscal or regulatory) *border* measure on the one hand or a (fiscal or regulatory) *domestic* measure on the other hand has considerable consequences for the leeway left to WTO Members, given that border measures violating Art. II or Art. XI are prohibited *per se* (unless they can exceptionally be justified in particular under Art. XX), whereas domestic measures falling under Art. III:2 or Art. III:4 are "merely" subject to a test of discrimination and are therefore in need of justification only if they turn out be discriminatory.[143] This is illustrated in the following Fig. 4.1.

As has also been explained above, the relationships between Art. II and Art. III:2 on the one hand and Art. III:4 and Art. XI on the other hand is regulated by the Note ad Art. III. The issue of how to categorize the CBAM is highly disputed, however. All of the four aforementioned alternatives have in fact been advocated in the literature.

The first possibility of categorizing the CBAM as a fiscal border measure coming under Art. II has been supported e.g. by *Quick* and *Bacchus*. Thus, *Quick* has argued that the EU ETS allowances system does not apply to products but to installations; CBAM, on the other hand, applies to products. In this view, the Note ad Art. III would not be applicable and the CBAM requirement to surrender certificates would therefore have to be assessed under Art. II:1(b) as a charge accruing on importation

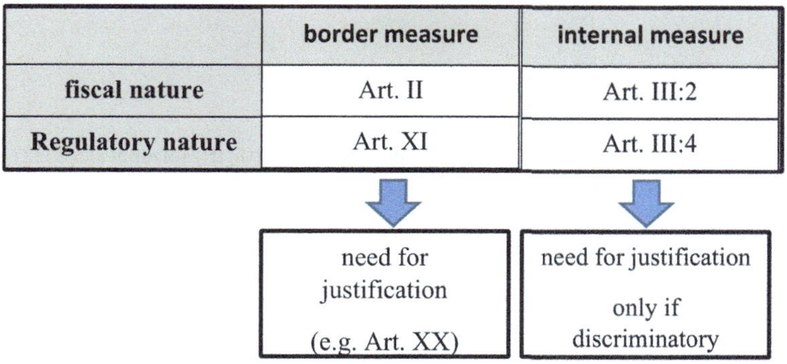

Fig. 4.1 Border vs internal measures, fiscal vs regulatory nature

[142] On this broad scope of Art. XI see above, Sect. 4.1.3.1.

[143] On this and the following see also Holzer et al. (2022), pp. 4–7.

("a payment at the border for a 'climate-sin' committed abroad").[144] Likewise, *Bacchus* classifies the obligation to surrender CBAM certificates as a charge imposed in connection with importation in terms of Art. II:1(b), given that this obligation, in his view, is not triggered by "an internal event such as the distribution [or] sale [...] of an imported product" in the sense of the WTO Appellate Body's aforementioned jurisprudence,[145] but accrues by virtue of the importation and due to the GHG emissions caused by production abroad.[146] However, this stance has been criticized as being too rigid on the basis that importation could also be seen as a mere prerequisite for the "internal distribution and sale of products" in the sense of the Appellate Body's approach.[147]

On the other hand, there are also voices in the literature in favor of the second alternative of classifying CBAM under Art. III:2.[148] In this perspective, the obligation to submit CBAM certificates is regarded as being caused by an *internal event*, namely the corresponding duty to buy ETS allowances for the production of goods covered by the EU ETS scheme.[149] Similarly, it has been submitted that the price of CBAM certificates being connected to the (average weekly) prices of ETS allowances[150] could at least *prima facie* militate for classifying the obligation to surrender CBAM certificates as a charge equivalent to an internal tax, which could render BTA under Art. III:2 possible.[151] However, as has also been emphasized, the ETS allowances scheme can hardly be subsumed under the OECD definition of taxes as "*unrequited* payments",[152] given that the purchase of ETS allowances can be considered as the *acquisition of the right* to emit given amounts of GHG.[153] In this view, a BTA relating to the CBAM would not be possible for lack of a corresponding internal tax measure. Furthermore, ETS allowances are tradable so that they could possibly even be categorized as goods in terms of the GATT or financial services in terms of the GATS Annex on Financial Services,[154] which also speaks against

[144] Quick (2020), pp. 563 ff (quote at 569).

[145] See above, Sect. 4.2.3.2.

[146] Bacchus (2021), p. 3; see also Hollaus and Mayr (2022), pp. 107 ff; Holzer et al. (2022), pp. 4 ff.

[147] Dobson (2022), p. 174.

[148] See e.g. Dobson (2022), pp. 174 ff.

[149] Holzer et al. (2022), pp. 4 ff.

[150] On this see above, Sect. 4.2.2.

[151] Hollaus and Mayr (2022), pp. 107 ff.

[152] Cf. OECD, Revenue Statistics. Interpretative Guide (available at https://www.oecd.org/content/dam/oecd/en/topics/policy-sub-issues/global-tax-revenues/oecd-classification-taxes-interpretative-guide.pdf): "In the OECD classification, the term 'taxes' is confined to compulsory unrequited payments to the general government or to a supranational authority. Taxes are unrequited in the sense that benefits provided by government to taxpayers are not normally in proportion to their payments" (p. 6).

[153] On this see also Quick (2020), p. 564; Dobson (2022), pp. 174 ff and Hollaus and Mayr (2022), pp. 107 ff.

[154] Cf. Vranes (2009d), pp. 707 ff, 715 ff.

regarding the ETS scheme as an internal tax measure, which would be the conceptual prerequisite for a BTA.

The third option, to consider the obligation to surrender CBAM certificates for imported goods as a quantitative restriction falling under Art. XI, has been rejected in academic writings on the ground that there is no quantitative limit on the amount of CBAM certificates that can be purchased.[155] However, as indicated before, pursuant to WTO jurisprudence the scope of Art. XI is comprehensive and extends beyond quantitative restrictions in a strict sense, as it applies to all measures other than measures taking the form of duties, taxes or other charges. Hence, the possibility that the CBAM is covered by Art. XI cannot be entirely ruled out.[156] In particular, it may be necessary to distinguish between the different elements of the CBAM, as some aspects of this mechanism could have to be scrutinized under Art. XI.[157]

As indicated above, the fourth alternative of regarding the CBAM as a mechanism falling under Art. III:4 has e.g. been advocated by the EU Commission[158] and has equally been discussed in academic writings.[159] Nonetheless, there are a number of differences between the ETS and the CBAM schemes: as pointed out above, the ETS applies to *installations*, whereas the CBAM is applicable to products; moreover, ETS allowances are tradable, which is not the case for CBAM certificates; additionally, the CBAM is charged on non-product-related process and production measures (so-called "npr ppm"[160]).[161] Consequently, it is questioned in the literature whether the CBAM could indeed be considered as the extension of an internal measure, namely the ETS scheme, for the purposes of Art. III:4.[162] On the other hand, it has been submitted that, although the ETS scheme applies to installations, it can nonetheless be regarded as being "sufficiently linked" to the *products* produced in the respective installations,[163] which would then make it possible to regard the CBAM as the extension of an internal measure in terms of Art. III:4.

---

[155] Hollaus and Mayr (2022), pp. 107 ff.

[156] This is also pointed out by Holzer et al. (2022), pp. 4 ff, 11 ff.

[157] Cf. Dobson (2022), pp. 174 ff; Holzer et al. (2022), pp. 4 ff, 11 ff; on this see also below, Sect. 4.2.3.4.3.

[158] See above, Sect. 4.2.1.

[159] Thus, as just mentioned, Hollaus and Mayr (2022), pp. 107 ff have taken the view that Art. III:4 may be applicable instead of Art XI given that the purchase of CBAM certificates is not subject to a quantitative ceiling.

[160] On this concept see above, Sect. 4.2.3.2.

[161] This is also emphasized by Holzer et al. (2022), pp. 4–7 und Quick (2020), pp. 563 ff.

[162] Cf. Quick (2020), p. 569.

[163] Englisch and Falcao (2021), pp. 10871, who argue that "the design of the ETS suggests that the pecuniary burden imposed through this system is *sufficiently linked* to the goods produced in the respective installations to qualify it as a charge that is imposed "with respect to the latter, rather than a charge merely imposed generally on a factor of production without a direct link to the production of a particular good. First, the need to acquire ETS allowances arises, and the corresponding costs are incurred, in the course of the production of a particular good, rather than at a prior stage that is not intrinsically linked to such a production process. Second, GHG-emitting production sites are per se covered by the ETS, but only if they are classified as installations where certain

Overall, there is no fully convincing solution as to how to categorize the CBAM. This conclusion is shared also by other authors.[164] Since there thus is no "black and white" answer to this question before relevant WTO rulings are issued, we will proceed as follows in the next (Sect. 4.2.3.4): we will first examine whether the CBAM may *prima facie* violate the GATT rules on customs duties (Sect. 4.2.3.4.1); next, it will be determined whether the CBAM could contravene the GATT prohibition on discriminatory tax treatment (Sect. 4.2.3.4.2); we will then assess whether the GATT prohibition on quantitative restrictions risks being infringed by the CBAM (Sect. 4.2.3.4.3) or whether the latter may also violate the GATT prohibition on discriminatory regulatory treatment (Sect. 4.2.3.4.). Finally, it will be determined whether the CBAM contravenes the GATT requirement of most-favoured-nation treatment (Sect. 4.2.3.4.5).

4.2.3.4 Potential Violations of the GATT

Upper Limits on Customs Duties (Art. II:1(b))

As has been explained above, Art. II:1(b) of the GATT lays down ceilings for customs duties and all other duties or charges (ODC) of any kind imposed on or in connection with importation. Thus, customs duties and ODC must not exceed the upper limits that a WTO Member has inscribed for given types of products in its country-specific schedule of tariff commitments. As has been clarified in WTO jurisprudence, the distinction between customs duties in the strict sense and ODC is not relevant as regards these upper limits, as the latter apply to both types of measure.[165] Against this backdrop, two aspects of the CBAM which may violate Art II:1(b) have been pointed out in the literature. First, if CBAM rates will not be recorded as customs duties or ODC in the EU's schedule of commitments, they will *per se* be inconsistent with Art. II:1(b).[166] Second, even if the CBAM were recorded in the EU's schedule, there is a clear risk that the upper limits, which are inscribed in this schedule on a product-specific basis, may be exceeded for given CBAM products due to the prices of CBAM certificates.[167]

---

specified goods are manufactured or produced, as laid down [in the EU ETS legal framework]. Against this background, the associated pecuniary burden can be adjusted in the case of like imported products, in conformity with GATT Art. II:2(a)" (italics added).

[164] Holzer et al. (2022), pp. 4 ff; Hollaus and Mayr (2022), pp. 107 ff.

[165] On this see also Quick (2020), pp. 578–579; Weiss et al. (2022), pp. 171–172 and 174.

[166] See Quick (2020), p. 579; on these issues in general see also Van den Bossche and Zdouc (2022), pp. 508 ff.

[167] Quick (2020), p. 579; Bacchus (2021), p. 3; Hollaus and Mayr (2022), pp. 109.

Differential Tax Treatment (Art. III:2)

Art. III:2 first sentence of the GATT requires WTO Members not to subject imported products to internal taxes or charges of any kind "in excess" of those applied to "like" domestic products. Pursuant to Art. III:2 second sentence, WTO Members must not otherwise apply internal taxation in a dissimilar manner to imported directly competitive or substitutable domestic (DCS) products.

As mentioned above, WTO dispute settlement practice has meanwhile clarified that the determination as to whether domestic and imported products are "like products" is to be based on the competitive relationship between the goods in question.[168] It is obvious that competition inherently depends on *consumer perception*: even products that differ in their physical appearance and in respect of other criteria may be competitive, if they are regarded as interchangeable to a sufficient degree by consumers; by the same token, products which appear quite similar with regard to criteria such as physical characteristics could nonetheless be treated as dissimilar and non-competitive by consumers.[169]

One consequence of this approach to likeness is of particular relevance for the CBAM, given that the CBAM relates to the GHG-intensity of the *processes* in which imported goods have been produced: It follows from this understanding of likeness that it appears possible that even *processing* methods—such as environmentally problematic methods – which are not physically ascertainable in the imported product, are regarded, by consumers, as rendering otherwise like products unlike.[170] Hence, it may be possible on this basis to argue in concrete cases that specific imported products, which are covered by the CBAM and stem from energy-intensive production methods, and similar domestic products, which are covered by the EU ETS and are produced in a more environmentally friendly manner, are not to be regarded as "like products" in terms of Art. III:2 first sentence. There would then be no violation of this GATT obligation.[171]

Furthermore, as has been pointed out by *Holzer, Espa* and *Cottier*, the WTO Appellate Body—in a ruling under the WTO Agreement on Subsidies and Countervailing Measures which was concerned with the competitive relationship between electricity generated from solar photovoltaic and wind power on the one hand and electricity generated from fossil fuels on the other hand—has found that these products were sold in different markets. Thus, if this approach were transposed to the determination of likeness, then carbon-intensive and low-carbon products could be found to be unlike products. Hence, in such cases there would be no violation of the non-discrimination disciplines in the GATT.[172] However, to the

[168] Cf. above, Sect. 4.1.3.1.

[169] Cf. Vranes (2009c), pp. 191 ff, 194 for a detailed discussion.

[170] Cf. Vranes (2009c), pp. 323–324 for a detailed discussion of, and further references on, this particular issue.

[171] See also Holzer et al. (2022), pp. 13 ff.

[172] Holzer et al. (2022), pp. 10–11, referring to the Appellate Body report, *Canada – Certain Measures Affecting the Renewable Energy Generation Sector* and *Canada – Measures Relating to*

extent that such products could be regarded as being in a looser competitive relationship than like products, they could possibly still be regarded as DCS products in concrete cases.[173]

On the other hand, if products are determined to be "like", then Art. III:2 first sentence, as just indicated, requires WTO Members not to subject imported products to internal taxes or charges of any kind "in excess" of those applied to like domestic products. According to the Appellate Body this means that "even the smallest amount" of higher taxation is prohibited. Furthermore, Art. III:2 first sentence is understood as requiring that actual tax burdens, as opposed to nominal tax rates, be compared. This provision is also read as not permitting WTO Members "to balance more favourable tax treatment of imported products in some instances against less favourable tax treatment of imported products in other instances".[174]

These guidelines are clearly relevant for our context. First, although the requirements under Art. III:2 appear strict, WTO jurisprudence has meanwhile refined and clarified the test of *de facto* discrimination under Art. III. Accordingly, WTO Members may draw regulatory distinctions between like products, as long as such differential treatment does not amount to a discrimination which preponderantly disadvantages foreign products. This means that one has to compare the treatment accorded to the two *entire groups* of like (or DCS) domestic products. Hence, the ratio between domestic favoured and disfavoured products must be roughly equivalent to the ratio between foreign favoured and disfavoured products.[175]

A second question again concerns the status of *process*-based measures such as the CBAM under the test of differential treatment under Art. III. In this regard, it is to be emphasized that a panel in 2000 found that *process*-based measures do not

---

the Feed-In Tariff Program, AB-2013-1, WT/DS412/AB/R, WT/DS426/AB/R, paras 5.167 ff.

[173] Cf. Holzer et al. (2022), pp. fn 38; as rightly underlined by these authors, regarding DCS products the standard of differential treatment is more lenient than the standard applicable to a differential treatment of like products. Thus, pursuant to Art. III:2 second sentence, WTO Members must not "otherwise apply" internal taxation in a dissimilar manner to imported DCS products. This has been interpreted in WTO jurisprudence as requiring a tax differential that is more than *de minimis*; moreover, there must not be dissimilar taxation of even some imported products as compared to DCS domestic products. Dissimilar taxation of DCS products is permissible, however, if it is not applied "so as to afford protection to domestic production'. This must primarily be ascertained by an examination of the design, architecture and structure of the national tax measure (WTO Appellate Body report, *Japan – Alcoholic Beverages II*, 27 ff; WTO Appellate Body report, *Canada – Certain Measures Concerning Periodicals,* WT/DS31/AB/R, adopted 30 July 1997, DSR 1997:I, p. 449, 29 ff; on all of this see also Van den Bossche and Zdouc (2022), pp. 403 ff; Vranes (2009c), pp. 240–249).

[174] On these issues see WTO Appellate Body report, *Japan – Alcoholic Beverages II*, 23; Panel Report, *Argentina – Measures Affecting the Export of Bovine Hides and the Import of Finished Leather*, WT/DS155/R and Corr.1, adopted 16 February 2001, DSR 2001:V, p. 1779, para 11.182 and para 11.260; see also Van den Bossche and Zdouc (2022), pp. 402 ff; Eichenberg (2010), pp. 315 ff.

[175] Appellate Body report, *European Communities – Measures Affecting Asbestos and Products Containing Asbestos,* WT/DS135/AB/R, adopted on 5 April 2001 (EC – Asbestos), para 100; for a detailed discussion cf. Ehring (2002), pp. 964 ff; Vranes (2009c) 238 ff.

constitute a special case under the standard of differential treatment.[176] Although this decision has been rendered under Art. I of the GATT, the panel's reasoning clearly appears transposable to Art. III and seems to be in conformity with academic writings according to which process-based measures should be regarded as being GATT-consistent, if they do not constitute (*de jure* or *de facto*) discriminatory measures.[177] With respect e.g. to environmental taxes, it has therefore been submitted that it is permissible to make distinctions on the basis of divergent process and production methods, so long as this does not amount to a disproportionate – i.e. *de facto* discriminatory – treatment of imported like products.[178]

Hence, while it is theoretically possible that a measure like the EU CBAM does not give rise to a finding of differential treatment in terms of Art. III, it is crucial that a finding of *de facto* discrimination hinges not only on the design of such a measure but also on its application and effects in concrete situations. In this context, academic writings have pointed to several aspects that could amount to discriminatory treatment of imported products under the CBAM. On the one hand, since the prices of CBAM certificates are connected to the *average* weekly prices of ETS allowances, there may be deviations negatively affecting imported products.[179] Furthermore, the fact that the ETS applies to producers (installations) whereas the CBAM applies to products could in concrete cases affect the competitive relationship between products subject to the CBAM and (like or DCS) domestic products subject to the ETS.[180] In addition, in cases where it turns out to be impossible or too burdensome for importers to state the actual emissions during the production of given imported products, importers may *de facto* be forced to rely on the alternative of using default values, which may negatively affect such imports.[181] Moreover, it has repeatedly been pointed out in the literature that the envisaged gradual phase-out of free allocations under the ETS scheme, which is to be coordinated with the phasing-in of the CBAM, could result in an (at least transitory) double protection of domestic products, if this coordination is not sufficiently synchronized, thereby risking to violate the national treatment principle.[182]

---

[176] Cf. Panel report, *Canada — Certain Measures Affecting the Automotive Industry*, WT/DS/142/R, adopted on 19 June 2000, para 10.25 ff.

[177] Cf. also Charnovitz (2002), pp. 61, 67 ff; see also Howse and Regan (2000), p. 252, who address this issue under Art. III of the GATT.

[178] See Low et al. (2012), p. 503; see also Hillman (2013), pp. 7 ff; Holzer and Shariff (2013), p. 249 ff; Pauwelyn (2012) 41 ff.

[179] This is also pointed out by Bacchus (2021), p. 3; Hollaus and Mayr (2022), pp. 109 ff.

[180] On this see Holzer et al. (2022), pp. 13 ff.

[181] See also Holzer et al. (2022), p. 18.

[182] Bacchus (2021), pp. 3 ff; Espa et al. (2022), pp. 16 ff; Holzer et al. (2022), p. 19; Hollaus and Mayr (2022), pp. 109 ff.

Quantitative Restrictions (Art. XI)

As stated above, WTO jurisprudence has interpreted the scope of Art. XI as being comprehensive and extending beyond quantitative restrictions in a strict sense, in that it has been held to apply to all measures other than measures taking the form of duties, taxes or other charges.[183] Against this background it has been argued that certain elements of the CBAM may be found to violate Art. XI, such as the considerable administrative burden imposed on importers to comply with the CBAM system, in particular as regards the reporting requirements relating to the actual amount of emissions that occurred during production.[184] Moreover, it has been argued that even if the CBAM were regarded as falling under Art. III:4,[185] elevated prices of CBAM certificates could additionally violate Art. XI, if they were found to *de facto* amount to import bans.[186]

Less Favourable Regulatory Treatment (Art. III:4)

According to Art. III:4 of the GATT, imported products must receive "treatment no less favourable" than "like" domestic products in respect of all national measures "affecting their internal sale, offering for sale, purchase, transportation, distribution or use".[187] Hence, just as under Art. III:2, the first criterion that must be assessed is that of "like products". Although the Appellate Body has cautioned that the notion of likeness (possibly) varies, its scope depending on the applicable GATT non-discrimination provision, its context and the concrete case,[188] the concept of likeness is interpreted, under Art. III:4 as well, as being concerned with the competitive relationship between imported and domestic products. Therefore, reference can be made to the considerations regarding Art. III:2, where it has been underlined that consumers may regard e.g. imported products produced in energy-intensive processes as being unlike domestic goods produced in low-carbon processes.[189]

The second central criterion under Art. III:4 is that of "less favourable treatment". This standard has meanwhile been clarified in WTO jurisprudence.[190] Furthermore, as has been explained above, differential treatment of imported and domestic like products, which is based on different production methods, does not amount to "less favourable treatment" in terms of the national treatment principle

---

[183] See above, Sect. 4.1.3.1.

[184] Cf. Dobson (2022), pp. 174 ff; Holzer et al. (2022), pp. 13 ff.

[185] On this possibility see the next subsection.

[186] Holzer et al. (2022), p. 20.

[187] On this see already above, Sect. 4.1.3.1.

[188] Appellate Body, *Japan–Taxes on Alcoholic Beverages,* WT/DS8/AB/R, WT/DS9/AB/R, WT/DS10/AB/R, adopted on 1 November 1996 (*Japan–Alcohol II*), Chap. H.1.

[189] Cf. above, Sect. 4.2.3.4.2.

[190] Cf. above, Sect. 4.1.3.1.

enshrined in Art. III, if such treatment does not disproportionally negatively affect imported products.[191]

As previously mentioned, several voices in the academic literature have submitted that at least certain aspects of the complex CBAM mechanism may have a regulatory nature in the sense of Art. III:4.[192] These authors basically point to issues that are similar to those which could be regarded as constituting unlawful differential treatment under Art. III:2 and could, by analogy, also been as violations of Art. III:4, in particular potential divergences in the prices of EU allowances and CBAM certificates;[193] the administrative burden of complying with the CBAM;[194] the fact that the ETS scheme applies to producers, whereas the CBAM applies to products;[195] negative competitive effects of possibly being required to use default values;[196] and potential distortions of competition caused during the overlap of the gradual phase-out of free allocations and the phase-in of the CBAM.[197]

Most-Favoured-Nation Treatment (Art. I)

According to Art. I of the GATT, WTO Members are obliged not to discriminate between products originating in different exporting countries. This applies not only to customs duties and charges imposed on or in connection with importation and exportation, but also to internal taxes in the sense of Art. III:2 as well as regulatory measures in terms of Art. III:4. As already explained above, Art. I comprises two basic tests: an examination as to whether the products that are treated differently are "like" products; and an examination as to whether such differential treatment amounts to (*de jure* or *de facto*) discriminatory treatment in the sense of Art. I.[198] Regarding both of these substantive requirements, reference can be made to the preceding sections on Art. III, given that these standards have been interpreted, under both Arts. I and III, in a similar manner in WTO jurisprudence and the academic literature.[199]

Crucially, the CBAM does not apply to products originating in countries to which the EU ETS applies or which have concluded an agreement with the EU fully linking their national emissions trading systems with the EU ETS.[200] This

[191] See above, Sect. 4.1.3.1.

[192] See e.g. Dobson (2022), p. 174 ff with further references.

[193] See Holzer et al. (2022), pp. 13 ff; Hollaus and Mayr (2022), pp. 109 ff.

[194] Dobson (2022), p. 174 ff.

[195] Holzer et al. (2022), pp. 13 ff.

[196] Holzer et al. (2022), pp. 13 ff.

[197] Bacchus (2021), pp. 3 ff; Holzer et al. (2022), pp. 13 ff, Hollaus and Mayr (2022), pp. 109 ff.

[198] Cf. above, Sect. 4.1.3.1.

[199] For a detailed analysis see also Vranes (2009c), pp. 250 ff with further references.

[200] Cf. above, Sect. 4.2.2.

derogation (which so far covers the EEA countries and Switzerland[201]), *prima facie* risks violating Art. I, as it favours products originating in these countries. As regards the EEA member states, it could possibly be justified under Art. XXIV of the GATT, which excludes free trade areas and customs unions from the scope of Art. I, if they substantially cover all trade in goods.[202] However, as argued by *Holzer*, *Espa* and *Cottier*, this defence may not be available with respect to the free trade agreement with Switzerland due to the restricted scope of application of the latter.[203]

Furthermore, Art. I may be infringed in a second, quite evident manner: while the CBAM makes it possible to reduce the number of certificates for imported products on the account of the carbon price already effectively paid in the country of origin,[204] this option is available only for goods having been subject to foreign *fiscal* measures. This clearly risks disfavouring goods originating in WTO Members which have taken equally or even more effective *non-fiscal* measures to address climate change.[205]

4.2.3.5 Justification of Violations of WTO Law

As the preceding Section has shown, there are clear risks that the CBAM may violate GATT disciplines. This Section therefore examines as to whether such prima facie violations could be justified under Art. XX, the general exceptions clause of the GATT.

General Remarks on Art. XX of the GATT

Within our context, Arts. XX(b) and XX(g) are primarily relevant: Art. XX(b) makes it possible to justify trade-restrictive measures that are "necessary to protect human, animal or plant life or health" (Art. XX(b)); similarly, Art. XX(g) can be invoked to defend measures "relating to the conservation of exhaustible natural resources". Moreover, Art. XX(d) may prove to be pertinent, given that it can be relied on to justify measures that are "necessary to secure compliance with laws or regulations which are not inconsistent with the provisions of [the GATT]". Furthermore, Art. XX(a) has been regarded as setting forth a ground of justification that could possibly be invoked, as it serves to justify measures "necessary to protect public morals".

Before we turn to these provisions, it should be underlined that WTO adjudicating bodies appear prepared to adopt a *broad interpretation* of relevant policy goals

---

[201] Cf. above, Sect. 4.2.2.

[202] Holzer et al. (2022), pp. 11 ff.

[203] Holzer et al. (2022), pp. 12–13.

[204] See above, Sect. 4.2.2.

[205] Dobson (2022), p. 175; Bacchus (2021), pp. 3 ff, Holzer et al. (2022), pp. 12–13.

laid down in Art. XX: thus, for example, "exhaustible resources" in Art. XX(g) has been understood by the Appellate Body as also covering renewable resources.[206] In the light of this approach, it seems evident that the planet's atmosphere, which is affected by climate change, qualifies as an exhaustible natural resource (and constitutes a precondition for the existence of other exhaustible natural resources) in the sense of Art. XX(g).[207]

It should also be stressed that the WTO adjudicating bodies have taken a rather ambiguous approach to the review of the *legitimacy* of the policy goal. On the one hand, panels have repeatedly underlined that it is not their task "to examine generally the desirability or necessity of the environmental objectives" of a WTO Member's measures.[208] On the other hand, however, several decisions have nonetheless implicitly or explicitly reviewed the legitimacy of the policy goal pursued by determining whether a stated policy falls within one of the categories set out in lit (b), (d) or (g) of Art. XX, and whether the value protected by these provisions is actually at risk in the given case.[209] It is apparent that considerable judicial deference has been applied in these cases.[210]

Likewise, the judicial approach to the level of protection sought by WTO Members invoking these exceptions has tended to be ambiguous. While panels and the Appellate Body have expressly held that establishing the appropriate level of protection in a concrete case "is a prerogative of the Member concerned and not of

[206] Appellate Body Report, *United States – Shrimp*, WT/DS58/AB/R, adopted 6 November 1998, DSR 1998:VII, p. 2755, paras 125 ff (in the following: *United States – Shrimp*).

[207] See also Pauwelyn (2012), p. 45.

[208] Cf. e.g. the Panel Report, *United States – Standards for Reformulated and Conventional Gasoline*, WT/DS2/R, adopted 20 May 1996, as modified by Appellate Body Report WT/DS2/AB/R, DSR 1996:I, p. 29, para 7.1; similarly, the panel in *US – Restrictions on Imports of Tuna*, DS21/R - 39S/155 (*US – Tuna I*), para 5.32 held that the conditions set out in Art. XX(g) do not relate to the conservation policies pursued by a contracting party, but merely to the measures adopted in pursuit of these goals.

[209] Cf. e.g. the panel report, *EC – Asbestos*, para 8.186, which held that "*in principle*, a policy that seeks to reduce exposure to a risk should fall within the range of policies designed to protect human life or health, *insofar as a risk exists*' (Panel Report, *European Communities – Measures Affecting Asbestos and Asbestos-Containing Products*, WT/DS135/R and Add.1, adopted 5 April 2001, as modified by Appellate Body Report WT/DS135/AB/R, DSR 2001:VIII, p. 3305); cf. also the panel report, *Thailand – Cigarettes*, para 73 (holding that "smoking constituted a serious risk to human health and *consequently* measures designed to reduce the consumption of cigarettes *fell within* the scope of Art. XX(b)"; Panel Report, *Thailand – Customs and Fiscal Measures on Cigarettes from the Philippines*, WT/DS371/R, adopted 15 July 2011, as modified by Appellate Body Report WT/DS371/AB/R, DSR 2011:IV, p. 2299); panel report, *US – Tuna II*, para 5.30 (holding that "the panel noted that the parties did not disagree that the protection of dolphin life or health was a policy that could come within Art. XX(b)"; GATT panel report, *US – Restrictions on Imports of Tuna*, DS29/R); panel report, *US – Gasoline*, para 6.21 (holding that it agreed "that the policy to reduce air pollution resulting from the consumption of gasoline was a policy within the range of those concerning the protection of human, animal and plant life or health mentioned in Art. XX(b)').

[210] Cf. panel report, *EC – Asbestos*, para 8.193. Cf. also Van den Bossche and Zdouc (2022), pp. 592 ff.

panels or the Appellate Body", the Appellate Body has nonetheless questioned the level of protection adopted in two ways. On the one hand, in *Korea - Beef* the Appellate Body has drawn an inference from the measure adopted to the presumable level of protection by the defendant.[211] On the other hand, this level has been determined by WTO adjudicating bodies themselves, when the defendant had not clearly stated the degree of protection sought.[212]

In this context, it has been noted that the CBAM pursues a variety of purposes, namely preventing carbon leakage (in order to make the EU's climate protection efforts more effective) as well as preserving a level playing field for domestic and imported products. However, as has also been emphasized, addressing the problem of carbon leakage is not possible without maintaining a level playing field. In line with relevant WTO jurisprudence,[213] since the environmental goal of CBAM clearly is the principal purpose of this mechanism, the level playing field concerns that are inextricably linked with this purpose should not *per se* disqualify the CBAM under the non-economic policy goals laid down in Art. XX(a), Art. XX(b), Art. XX(d) and Art. XX(g).[214]

Furthermore, it should be pointed out that WTO jurisprudence so far has not given a clear-cut answer to the fundamental question as to whether unilateral trade measures, which address environmental concerns that are located abroad, can possibly be justified under Art. XX. The Appellate Body has emphasized, however, in *US – Shrimp* and more recently in *EC – Seal* that such justification may be possible, if there is a "sufficient nexus" between conduct occurring abroad and domestic legitimate concerns.[215]

In the following Sections, we will proceed as follows: We will first turn to Art. XX(b) and Art. XX(d), both of which contain a "necessity" requirement. We will then deal with Art. XX(a), which also sets forth this requirement, but has only rather recently been invoked in jurisprudence and should therefore be interpreted against the background of WTO dispute settlement practice relating to Art. XX(b) and Art. XX(d). We will then address Art. XX(g), which is not based on the "necessity" test, but on the concept "*relating to* [...] exhaustible natural resources". Finally, we will examine the relevance of the Chapeau of Art. XX for the design and application of the CBAM.

---

[211] Appellate Body report, *Korea – Beef*, para 178.

[212] On this cf. Vranes (2009c), pp. 265–266 with further references.

[213] Appellate Body report, *EC - Seal*, para 5.167.

[214] Holzer et al. (2022), pp. 21.

[215] Appellate Body report, *US – Shrimp*, para 133; Appellate Body report, *EC - Seal*, para 5.173; see also Van den Bossche and Zdouc (2022), p. 600.

Protection of Human, Animal or Plant Life or Health (Art. XX(b))

Under Art. XX(b), it must be shown that a measure is "necessary to protect human, animal or plant life or health". A WTO panel has ruled that, as regards the objective of environmental policy measures, a WTO Member must "establish the existence not just of risks to 'the environment' generally, but specifically of risks to animal or plant life or health".[216] As indicated, it seems evident that this condition is fulfilled as regards the many significant risks posed by climate change, such as heat waves, floods and storms, which are to be addressed through the CBAM.[217]

WTO dispute settlement practice also inquires into whether a measure is "designed to" protect human, animal or plant life or health. This standard tends to constitute no considerable hurdle, since WTO jurisprudence merely examines whether the measure to be justified is "not incapable of contributing to" the policy objectives pursued by this means.[218]

Turning to the pivotal criterion "necessary to", it should be noted that the necessity requirements under Arts. XX(b) and (d) have been applied in a largely analogous manner. The WTO's current approach to the necessity requirement was introduced into WTO jurisprudence in 2000 in *Korea – Beef*, a decision concerned with Art. XX(d).[219] This approach has been transferred to Art. XX(b) by the Appellate Body in *EC – Asbestos*, where it has held that the more important the value pursued by a measure and the more a measure contributes to the protection of this value, the more easily the measure may be considered to be "necessary".[220] Furthermore, it has emphasized that the preservation of human life and health is a value that is "both vital and important in the highest degree".[221]

Regarding the analysis of the contribution of a measure to the goal pursued, the Appellate Body made several clarifying statements in *EC – Seal*, holding that this analysis can be quantitative or qualitative in nature,[222] that it is sufficient that a measure is "*apt* to make a contribution *in the future*",[223] and that there is no general requirement that the contribution be "significant" in general, as this threshold is to be determined depending on the concrete circumstances of individual cases.[224]

If an analysis of these factors—i.e. the importance of the values at stake, the extent of the contribution to the achievement of the measure's objective, and its

[216] Panel report, *Brazil – Measures Affecting Imports of Retreaded Tyres*, WT/DS332/R, adopted 17 December 2007, as modified by Appellate Body Report WT/DS332/AB/R, DSR 2007:V, p. 1649. (*Brazil – Retreaded Tyres*), para 7.46.

[217] See also Holzer et al. (2022), pp. 22.

[218] Cf. Van den Bossche and Zdouc (2022), pp. 607 ff with further references to WTO jurisprudence.

[219] Appellate Body report, *Korea – Beef*, paras 152 ff.

[220] Appellate Body report, *EC – Asbestos*, para 172.

[221] Appellate Body report, *EC – Asbestos*, para 172.

[222] Appellate Body report, *EC – Seal*, para 5.211.

[223] Appellate Body report, *EC – Seal*, para 5.213.

[224] Appellate Body report, *EC – Seal*, para 5.213.

trade restrictiveness—makes a measure appear necessary *prima facie*, then "this result must be confirmed by comparing the measure with possible *alternatives*, which may be less trade restrictive while providing an equivalent contribution to the achievement of the objective. This comparison should be carried out in the light of the importance of the interests or values at stake. It is through this process that a panel determines whether a measure is necessary".[225] In determining whether such an alternative is reasonably available, "one aspect [...] is the extent to which the alternative measure 'contributes to the realization of the end pursued'."[226] If the alternative is not suitable to achieve the desired level of protection, a WTO Member cannot be expected to employ it. Furthermore, an alternative measure is not "reasonably available", if it is merely theoretical, "for instance, where the responding Member is not capable of taking it, or where the measure imposes an undue burden on that Member, such as prohibitive costs or substantial technical difficulties".[227]

Applying this necessity analysis to the CBAM, it has been argued that there would be a less trade-restrictive alternative, namely the introduction of a carbon tax.[228] However, the EU Commission has submitted on the basis of an impact assessment that this alternative would be less effective in preventing carbon leakage.[229] Against the backdrop of the WTO case law just referred to, the potential alternative of a carbon tax would therefore not necessarily be regarded as being "reasonably available". On the other hand, it has been submitted that estimates of the contribution of the EU CBAM to the prevention of carbon leakage would be helpful in arguing that the "necessity" requirement, as interpreted in WTO jurisprudence, is fulfilled.[230] However, in the light of the WTO dispute settlement practice just referred to, it is sufficient that a measure addresses the "risk" of carbon leakage;[231] moreover, the possibility that carbon leakage may arise without a mechanism such as the CBAM is recognized by scholars as a *real* risk.[232]

Furthermore, commentators have argued that the largest producers of emissions are not necessarily the EU's largest suppliers; and producers situated in third countries may simply decide to export carbon-intensive products to other non-EU-countries. Hence, the leverage of the EU market may not be strong enough to exert decisive influence on production processes in third countries.[233] This objection,

---

[225] Appellate Body report, *Brazil – Measures Affecting Imports of Retreaded Tyres*, WT/DS332/AB/R, adopted 17 December 2007, DSR 2007:IV, p. 1527 (*Brazil – Retreaded Tyres*), para 178.

[226] Appellate Body report, *EC – Asbestos*, para 172. On all of this see also the overview provided in Van den Bossche and Zdouc (2022), pp. 608 ff.

[227] Appellate Body report, *Brazil – Retreaded Tyres*, para 156. Appellate Body report, *EC – Seal*, para 5.261; on all of this see also the overview provided in Van den Bossche and Zdouc (2022), pp. 608 ff.

[228] Bacchus (2021), p. 4.

[229] Cf. Hollaus and Mayr (2022), pp. 112.

[230] Holzer et al. (2022), p. 23.

[231] Dobson (2022), p. 177.

[232] Espa et al. (2022), pp. 11–12.

[233] Erixon (2022), pp. 55–56.

which relates to the question of the suitability of the CBAM to "contribute" to the promotion of the EU's policy goal, arguably does not preclude justification under Art. XX(b), given that it is sufficient, as just indicated, that a measure is "*apt* to make a contribution *in the future*", and that there is no general requirement that the contribution be "significant" in general.[234]

Hence, in the light of the balancing required by WTO dispute settlement practice under the "necessity" test and given that (i) climate mitigation pursues a value—the preservation of human life and health—which, in the Appellate Body's words, is "vital and important in the highest degree",[235] (ii) that the CBAM is regarded as not being incapable of making a contribution to the furtherance of this goal, and (iii) that the trade effects of the CBAM may be lower than that of other trade restrictions, the CBAM arguably stands a good chance of surviving examination under Art. XX(b).

Measures Necessary to Secure Compliance with Domestic Law (Art. XX(d))

Under Art. XX(d) of the GATT, it must be shown that a measure is "*necessary* to secure compliance with laws or regulations which are not inconsistent" with the GATT. Importantly, Art. XX(d) does not set forth an exhaustive list of policy goals.[236] Relevant case law has been read as making it possible to justify measures the "overall objective" of which is compatible with the GATT. Against this background, it has been submitted that Art. XX(d) could be invoked with respect to the EU CBAM, since its objective clearly is compatible with the goals of sustainable development and the protection of natural resources, which are also highlighted in the Preamble of the WTO Agreement.[237] As has been described above, the "necessity" test, which is also part of Art. XX(d), has been developed in a mostly analogous manner under Art. XX(b) and Art. XX(d). Hence, if the CBAM is regarded as being justified under Art. XX(b) or Art. XX(d), then it is likely to also pass scrutiny under Art. XX(d).

Protection of Public Morals (Art. XX(a))

According to Art. XX(a) of the GATT, WTO Members can justify measures that are found to be "necessary to protect public morals". WTO case law has recognized that the concept of "public morals" can vary from Member to Member and that individual WTO Members have to be granted leeway to define the concept of public morals, the level of protection sought as well as how this concept should be

234 Appellate Body report, *EC – Seal*, para 5.213.

235 Appellate Body report, *EC – Asbestos*, para 172.

236 See also Van den Bossche and Zdouc (2022), pp. 614 ff.

237 Holzer et al. (2022), p. 23.

applied.[238] Similarly to its approach to Art. XX(b) and Art. XX(d), WTO jurisprudence under Art. XX(a) assesses whether a measure is "designed to" promote the policy goal pursued ("public morals") and likewise confines itself to ascertaining whether the measure at issue is not "incapable" of furthering this objective.[239] As explained above, Art. XX(a) also encompasses a "necessity" test, which is applied in WTO jurisprudence in a similar manner as under Art. XX(b) and Art. XX(d).[240] On this basis and as has been argued in the literature, it may indeed be possible to invoke Art. XX(a) to justify the CBAM on grounds of intergenerational equity concerns.[241]

Conservation of Exhaustible Natural Resources (Art. XX(g))

Art. XX(g) requires that a measure, for which justification is sought, be (1) "*relating to* the conservation of exhaustible resources" and (2) be "made effective *in conjunction with* restrictions on domestic production or consumption".

According to the Appellate Body, the "relating to" standard has come to be understood to designate a "close and genuine relationship of ends and means",[242] in which the measure at issue is not "merely incidentally or inadvertently aimed at the conservation" of an exhaustible resource.[243] The Appellate Body examines the design and structure of the measure at issue as well as its predictable effects.[244] A deferential approach has been applied with regard to these standards.[245]

On the other hand, "in conjunction with" is read as implying an "even-handedness in the imposition of restrictions". This consistency requirement, however, is not meant to require "identical treatment of domestic and imported products".[246] According to the Appellate Body, "made effective in conjunction with" does not mean that the defendant must prove that is has taken a given measure so as to render effective restrictions which are imposed on domestic production or consumption. It

[238] Cf. Van den Bossche and Zdouc (2022), pp. 629 ff summarizing relevant WTO jurisprudence.

[239] Van den Bossche and Zdouc (2022), p. 636.

[240] On this cf. above, Sect. 4.2.3.5.1.

[241] See Holzer et al. (2022), p. 23, referring additionally to pending WTO cases.

[242] Appellate Body Report, *US – Shrimp*, para 136.

[243] Appellate Body Report, *United States – Gasoline*, WT/DS2/AB/R, adopted 20 May 1996, DSR 1996:I, p. 19.

[244] Appellate Body Report, Appellate Body Reports, *China – Measures Related to the Exportation of Rare Earths, Tungsten, and Molybdenum*, WT/DS431/AB/R / WT/DS432/AB/R / WT/DS433/AB/R, adopted 29 August 2014, DSR 2014:III, p. 805 (*China – Rare Earths*), paras 5.111 and 5.113.

[245] This ensues from the Appellate Body's emphasizing that these standards are violated only if a specific measure "cannot in any possible situation have any positive effect on conservation goals' (cf. the Appellate Body Report, *United States – Gasoline*, WT/DS2/AB/R, adopted 20 May 1996, DSR 1996:I, p. 21).

[246] Appellate Body Report, *United States – Gasoline*, WT/DS2/AB/R, adopted 20 May 1996, DSR 1996:I, p. 20.

is sufficient for a defendant WTO Member to show that its measures "work together with restrictions on domestic production or consumption, which operate so as to conserve an exhaustible natural resource".[247]

As regards the EU CBAM, it seems obvious that there is a "close and genuine relationship", in the sense of the Appellate Body's interpretation of these terms and in the light of its deferential approach, between the means of the CBAM and the objective of protecting the climate and exhaustible resources. Likewise, the condition that the means of the CBAM be "made effective in conjunction with restrictions on domestic production and consumption" seems fulfilled as it "work[s] together" with the EU's ETS mechanism, i.e., to use the words of the Appellate Body again, with "restrictions on domestic production or consumption, which operate so as to conserve an exhaustible natural resource".[248] Hence, it is not unlikely that the CBAM could be provisionally justified also under Art. XX(g).

Justification Under the Chapeau of Art. XX

If it has been shown that a given measure is provisionally justified under one of the individual paragraphs of Art. XX, then it must still be demonstrated that it is also in line with the Chapeau of Art. XX. In fact, most attempts to invoke Art. XX as a defence so far have failed to overcome the requirements inferred from the Chapeau in WTO jurisprudence.[249]

According to the Chapeau, a trade measure must not be "*applied* in a manner which would constitute a means of *arbitrary* or *unjustifiable discrimination* between countries where the same conditions prevail, or a *disguised restriction* on international trade" (emphasis added). It has proven difficult to draw clear dividing lines between these three concepts based on their wording, systematic-teleological considerations and the drafting history of this provision. Rather, these interpretative

---

[247] See Appellate Body Reports, *China – Measures Related to the Exportation of Various Raw Materials*, WT/DS394/AB/R / WT/DS395/AB/R / WT/DS398/AB/R, adopted 22 February 2012, DSR 2012:VII, p. 3295 (*China – Raw Materials*), para 356; on this see also Van den Bossche and Zdouc (2022), pp. 624 ff. The Appellate Body further found that "'the clause 'made effective in conjunction with restrictions on domestic production or consumption' requires that, when GATT-inconsistent measures are in place, effective restrictions must also be imposed on domestic production or consumption. Just as GATT-inconsistent measures impose limitations on international trade, domestic restrictions must impose limitations on domestic production or consumption. Such restrictions must be 'real' rather than existing merely 'on the books', particularly in circumstances where domestic consumption accounts for a major part of the exhaustible natural resources to be conserved. Moreover, such restrictions on domestic production or consumption must reinforce and complement the restriction on international trade. However, we have also clarified that Art. XX(g) does not require a Member seeking to justify its measure to establish that its regulatory regime achieves an even distribution of the burden of conservation" (Appellate Body report, *China – Rare Earths*, para 5.136).

[248] See Appellate Body reports, *China – Raw Materials*, para 356; see also Holzer et al. (2022), pp. 21–22; Hollaus and Mayr (2022), pp. 111 ff.

[249] Weiss et al. (2022), pp. 206 ff; on the following see also Vranes (2009c), pp. 278 ff.

efforts have resulted in the identification of a common "fundamental theme" which is that of "avoiding abuse or illegitimate use" of Art. XX.[250] The Appellate Body has defined this prohibition on abuse of rights as demanding that measures to be justified "must be applied reasonably, with due regard both to the legal duties of the party claiming the exception and the legal rights of the other parties concerned",[251] which essentially means that a "balance of rights and obligations"—and thereby of trade and other concerns—must be struck under the Chapeau.[252]

The leading decisions in the context of trade and environmental protection have been issued in the *US – Shrimp* proceedings in particular. In this regard, the Appellate Body has held that "arbitrary and unjustifiable discrimination" can occur when a WTO Member "require[s] other Members to adopt essentially the same comprehensive program [...] without taking into considerations different conditions which may occur in the territories of those other Members".[253] Discrimination can be found to be "arbitrary and unjustifiable" in especially "when the application of the measure at issue does not allow for any inquiry into the appropriateness of the regulatory program for the conditions prevailing in those exporting countries".[254] Such arbitrary discrimination arises in particular, when a WTO Member "imposes a single, rigid and unbending requirement" for other Members to adopt essentially the same program as its own.[255] According to the Appellate Body, WTO Members ought to recognize foreign programs that are "comparable in effectiveness".[256]

Furthermore, the Appellate Body has held that discrimination may be found to be "unjustifiable" when the discriminatory effects were foreseeable and were "not merely inadvertent or unavoidable".[257] Additionally, the Appellate Body has found that an importing Member is required "to engage [...] in serious, across-the-board negotiations" before imposing unilateral trade-restrictive measures.[258] This requirement is seen as applying in particular when the "very policy objective of the measure [...] demands concerted and cooperative efforts."[259]

In view of these judicial guidelines, it does not come as a surprise that several exporting countries and scholars have argued that the CBAM can hardly be justified under the Chapeau. Thus, it has been submitted that there have been no sufficient

[250] Appellate Body Report, *United States – Gasoline*, WT/DS2/AB/R, adopted 20 May 1996, DSR 1996:I, p. 3, p. 22.

[251] Ibidem, p. 22.

[252] Appellate Body Report, *United States – Shrimp*, paras 152–159.

[253] Appellate Body Report, *United States – Shrimp*, para 164.

[254] Appellate Body Report, *United States – Shrimp*, para 165.

[255] Appellate Body Report, para 177.

[256] Appellate Body Report, *United States – Shrimp*, WT/DS58/AB/RW (Recourse to Art. 21.5 of the DSU by Malaysia), para 144.

[257] Appellate Body Report, *United States – Gasoline*, WT/DS2/AB/R, adopted 20 May 1996, DSR 1996:I, pp. 28 ff.

[258] Appellate Body Report, *United States – Shrimp*, para 166.

[259] Van den Bossche and Zdouc (2022), p. 651.

efforts of prior negotiations by the EU with other WTO Members.[260] Moreover, it has been suggested that the EU imposes its own standards on other countries[261] and does so in a coercive manner,[262] in especially without taking into account non-price-based efforts to mitigate climate change that have been taken by other WTO Members.[263] Using the words of the Appellate Body, the EU requires other WTO Members to "adopt essentially the same program" as itself without recognizing that non-price-based measures can be "comparable in effectiveness" and should be recognized, therefore.[264] Moreover, it has repeatedly been pointed out that the EU may be required, under the Chapeau and WTO law as well as under international environmental law more generally, to accord more favourable treatment to developing countries.[265]

Despite these arguments, there could be a glimmer of hope for the EU under the Chapeau, if it could successfully argue that the countries treated differently under the CBAM are countries where different conditions prevail. There would then be no discriminatory treatment.[266] However, this type of argument, which has been regarded as questionable in the CBAM context,[267] has not succeeded in WTO jurisprudence so far.[268]

4.3 The EU's Foreign Subsidies Regulation and WTO Law

The third horizontal instrument that is perceived as being required to shield the EU's Internal Energy Market vis à vis third states is the EU's Foreign Subsidies Regulation. This Chapter first briefly explains the relevance of foreign subsidies for the energy sector (Sect. 4.3.1), before it outlines the EU Foreign Subsidies Regulation (Sect. 4.3.2). It then examines to what extent this regulation risks violating fundamental WTO disciplines as laid down in the WTO Agreement on Subsidies and Countervailing Measures (ASCM) and the GATS and whether any prima facie violations of WTO rules could be justified under the general exceptions of the GATT and GATS Agreements (Sect. 4.3.3).

---

[260] Quick (2020), pp. 579 ff; Holzer et al. (2022), p. 28.

[261] Bacchus (2021), p. 5.

[262] Cf. the statement by India in the WTO Committee on Market Access, Minutes of 16 and 17 October 2023, WTO document G/MA/M/79 of 5 February 2024.

[263] Quick (2020), pp. 579 ff, Hollaus and Mayr (2022), pp. 111 ff; see also the statement by Paraguay in the WTO Committee on Market Access, Minutes of 16 and 17 October 2023, WTO document G/MA/M/79 of 5 February 2024.

[264] Holzer et al. (2022), pp. 20 ff.

[265] Dobson (2022), p. 178; see also Holzer et al. (2022), pp. 20 ff; Quick (2020), pp. 579 ff.

[266] Pauwelyn and Kleimann (2020), p. 11; on this see also Dobson (2022), p. 177.

[267] Dobson (2022), p. 177.

[268] Van den Bossche and Zdouc (2022), pp. 655.

4.3.1 Foreign Subsidies and the Energy Sector

4.3.1.1 Recent Developments

Subsidies had long been seen as a tool to stimulate economic growth in domestic sectors, although various types of subsidies—such as export buyer credit schemes—already had had transborder dimensions for a considerable time.[269] Such "extraterritorial" or cross-border subsidies have typically been provided by industrialized to developing countries, with Western state-owned enterprises active in developing countries having often been the recipients of such subsidies.[270] Today, however, developing countries, and China in particular, are increasingly providing cross-border subsidies to companies based in developed countries.[271] In addition, developed countries and the EU fear that countries such as the US and the UK will likewise increasingly grant cross-border subsidies to companies based in other countries or in the EU Internal Market.[272] This change in the economic landscape has raised concerns that some donor countries may be pursuing not only "purely" economic, but also strategic objectives, such as the acquisition of critical infrastructure and access to high technology abroad.[273]

In terms of terminology, it is useful to distinguish two types of "extraterritorial" subsidies: On the one hand, a state may grant subsidies to enterprises established in another country. In line with *Crochet* and *Gustafsson* and other authors as well, subsidies of this kind, which are granted in a bilateral relationship between two states, will be referred to in the following as "foreign subsidies". On the other hand, a state may provide financial support to companies in another state, which may then export products to a third country. Subsidies of this type, which thus occur in a relationship between three states, will be referred to in this Chapter as "transnational subsidies".[274] Although both types of subsidies can be problematic from an economic viewpoint, this distinction is useful from a legal point of view, as the EU's Foreign Subsidies Regulation (FSR) only applies to "foreign subsidies" as just defined.[275]

---

[269] On this and the following cf. in particular Crochet and Hegde (2020), pp. 1 ff; Crochet and Gustafsson (2021), pp. 344 ff.

[270] Crochet and Gustafsson (2021), p. 345.

[271] See also Tokas (2022), pp. 779 ff.

[272] Crochet and Gustafsson (2021), pp. 344 ff; EU Commission, White Paper on levelling the playing field as regards foreign subsidies, 17 June 2020, COM(2020)253 final.

[273] Crochet and Gustafsson (2021), pp. 344 ff; EU Commission, White Paper on levelling the playing field as regards foreign subsidies, 17 June 2020, COM(2020)253 final, pp. 6 ff.

[274] This terminology is also adopted by Crochet and Hegde (2020), pp. 1 ff; Crochet and Gustafsson (2021), p. 344; Nagy (2023), p. 890–891.

[275] See below, Sect. 4.3.2.

In a 2020 White Paper preceding the enactment of the FSR, the EU Commission explained why it considered foreign subsidies to be particularly problematic.[276] On the one hand, the Commission argues that foreign subsidies can distort the conditions of competition in the Internal Market. In this respect, it points to an increasing number of cases where foreign subsidies have allegedly facilitated the acquisition of EU companies by foreign investors, have otherwise influenced investment decisions or have distorted the market behaviour of the recipients of such subsidies.[277] The White Paper stresses that many subsidies of this type would be illegal if granted by an EU Member State and assessed under EU state aid rules. However, these rules do not apply to foreign subsidies offered by third countries. Against this background, the Commission argues that such subsidies create an uneven playing field, risk triggering subsidy races and may lead to the acquisition of EU targets through outbidding by foreign investors, who could thereby gain control e.g. over critical infrastructure and sensitive technologies. In addition, foreign subsidies could distort public procurement and access to funding programs in the EU.[278]

In the *energy* context, foreign subsidies may turn out to be particularly worrisome. As has been argued by analysts, the major global economies fiercely compete to boost renewable energy through subsidies.[279] Thus, China is regarded as the largest producer of green energy in the world already, a position achieved not least through massive subsidization. The US, on the other hand, has reacted to this challenge by adopting the Inflation Reduction Act, which is geared in particular towards green energy. This, in turn, has contributed to the EU's decision to launch the Green Deal, which likewise is meant to promote the transition to green energy. Hence, there is a clear risk of a *subsidies* war relating to green *energy*.[280]

Therefore, the EU FSR is particularly important in the energy context. This is also borne out by the application of the FSR in the first months after its entry into force, as there is a clear focus on the energy sector in the EU Commission's practice so far, as evidenced by the fact that of the first six investigations under the FSR, three concerned the energy sector: thus, one *ex officio* investigation concerned foreign subsidies for wind turbines in Bulgaria, France, Greece, Romania and Spain, while two in-depth investigations have focused on foreign subsidies for solar photovoltaic supplies in Romania and electric trains in Bulgaria.[281] It is also striking that all but one of the in-depth and *ex officio* investigations in this initial phase have targeted Chinese companies.[282]

---

[276] EU Commission, White Paper on levelling the playing field as regards foreign subsidies, 17 June 2020, COM(2020)253 final.

[277] EU Commission, White Paper on levelling the playing field as regards foreign subsidies, 17 June 2020, COM(2020)253 final, p. 4.

[278] EU Commission, White Paper on levelling the playing field as regards foreign subsidies, 17 June 2020, COM(2020)253 final, pp. 5 ff.

[279] Gam and Papaefthymiou (2023), pp. 3 ff.

[280] Gam and Papaefthymiou (2023), pp. 3–4.

[281] Cleary Gottlieb (2024).

[282] Cleary Gottlieb (2024).

4.3.1.2 Existence of a "Regulatory Gap"?

The motivation for the EU to adopt the FSR is a perceived "regulatory gap" that according to the EU Commission exists both on the levels of EU and international law. As explained by the Commission's White Paper, on the level of EU law, antitrust and merger control rules do not specifically take into account foreign subsidies. Moreover, EU state aid rules, as mentioned above, do no apply to foreign subsidies. Likewise, the EU's new FDI Screening Regulation does not specifically deal with foreign subsidies.[283]

At the level of WTO law, on the other hand, there evidently exists a lacuna in that the scope of the WTO Agreement on Subsidies and Countervailing Measures (ASCM) is limited to goods.[284] Furthermore, as regards *foreign* subsidies relating to goods, the WTO Expert Group on Trade Financing has noted that "it is not entirely clear whether or not the [ASCM] applies where the subsidizing entity is not within the territory of the Member whose goods are allegedly being subsidize".[285] In addition, the GATS merely contains a hortatory clause according to which a Member that considers itself to be affected by a subsidy granted by another Member may request consultations on such matters. However, such requests should only be given "sympathetic consideration".[286] Substantive disciplines should have been negotiated by the Members of the WTO in the GATS context pursuant to Art. XV of the GATS, but no such rules have yet been adopted.[287] Hence, there are no rules on the level of WTO law disciplining subsidies granted for services and investors providing services (suppliers of services through "commercial presence" in the sense of Art. I.2(c) of the GATS[288]).

Against this background two fundamental issues need to be examined: that is, first, the question as to whether the view of the Commission regarding the perceived gap in WTO law is correct; and second, whether the EU FSR and its application can close the gap, to the extent it actually exists, in a WTO-compliant manner.

We will address these two questions in Sect. 4.3.3. Before doing so, it is appropriate to briefly outline the EU FSR and the ASCM.

---

[283] EU Commission, White Paper on levelling the playing field as regards foreign subsidies, 17 June 2020, COM(2020)253 final, pp. 9 ff; on this see e.g. also Frank (2023), pp. 938 ff.

[284] See infra, Sect. 4.3.3.1.

[285] Cf. WTO General Council, Working Group on Trade, Debt and Finance. WTO document WT/GC/W/527, WT/WGTDF/W/22, 16 March 2004; on this see also Crochet and Hegde (2020), pp. 1 ff; Gam and Papaefthymiou (2023), pp. 4 ff.

[286] Art. XV(2) of the GATS.

[287] EU Commission, White Paper on levelling the playing field as regards foreign subsidies, 17 June 2020, COM(2020)253 final, pp. 9 ff; Frank (2023), pp. 938 ff.

[288] On the concept of "commercial presence" see already above, Sect. 4.1.3.2.

4.3.2 The EU Foreign Subsidies Regulation Outlined

According to Art. 1 of the FSR, the FSR is meant to address foreign subsidies that may cause distortions in the EU Internal Market arising from any economic activity.[289] It therefore applies to foreign subsidies that are granted to companies (including public undertakings controlled directly or indirectly by a State) engaging in economic activities in the EU.[290] Undertakings acquiring control of or merging with a company established in the Internal Market as well as undertakings participating in public procurement in the EU are considered to be engaging in an economic activity in the EU Internal Market.[291] It follows from the wording of Art. 1 that the FSR does not apply to "*transnational* subsidies" in the sense defined above.[292] It should be noted, moreover, that the FSR applies to both EU-owned and multinational (foreign-owned) undertakings that receive subsidies from third countries.[293]

The FSR defines "*foreign* subsidies" as financial contributions provided directly or indirectly by a third country that confer a benefit on undertakings as defined above and which are *de jure* or *de facto* limited to one or more undertakings or industries.[294] Financial contributions in the sense of the FSR are defined in a non-exhaustive manner as including *inter alia* the transfer of funds or liabilities (such as capital injections, grants, loans and other instruments), the foregoing of revenue that is otherwise due and the provision, or purchase, of goods or services.[295] Relevant financial contributions can be provided by the central government and public authorities at all other levels of a third country as well as foreign public and private entities that can be attributed to a third State. Hence, while there are overlaps with relevant definitions in the WTO ASCM,[296] these FSR-specific definitions are broader in reach.[297]

---

[289] Art. 1(1) of the FSR.

[290] Art. 1(2) of the FSR.

[291] Art. 1(2) of the FSR.

[292] See also Nagy (2023), p. 893. The reason for this arguably is that the EU Commission and the ECJ have attributed transnational subsidies to the exporting country. The leading case in this regard is the "Glass Fibres" case, in which China, having established an exclusive economic zone (EEZ) in Egypt, granted financial contributions to companies based in this EEZ. When these companies then exported glass fibres to the EU, the EU Commission and the ECJ attributed the subsidies received by these companies to Egypt as the exporting country. Therefore, the Commission and the ECJ applied the EU's Anti-Subsidy Regulation (which implements the WTO ASCM Agreement) to this case (cf ECJ, joined cases C-269/23 P and C-272/23 P, *Hengshi Egypt Fiberglass Fabrics SAE and Jushi Egypt for Fiberglass Industry SAE v European Commission*, ECLI:EU:C:2024:984). If one adopts this—controversial—viewpoint, then there may indeed be no need to extend the scope of the FSR to such trilateral relationships. On these issues see also Crochet and Hegde (2020); Ding Ru and Yiqian (2022), pp. 48 ff.

[293] Nagy (2023), p. 897.

[294] Art. 3(1) of the FSR.

[295] Art. 3(2) of the FSR.

[296] Cf. below, Sect. 4.3.3.1.

[297] Cf. also Herrmann and Ellemann (2024), pp. 75–76.

Whether a distortion of the market exists is to be assessed on the basis of an indicative set of criteria such as the amount and nature of the foreign subsidy.[298] Certain categories of foreign subsidies—such as subsidies directly facilitating a merger—are deemed to "most likely distort" the Internal Market.[299] When the EU Commission decides whether to impose measures against foreign subsidies, it must undertake a balancing test, in which it has to weigh up the negative and positive effects of a given foreign subsidy.[300]

Measures taken against foreign subsidies include redressive measures as well as commitments that may be offered by an undertaking under investigation by the EU Commission. Redressive measures and commitments may consist of a series of instruments that are enumerated in a non-exhaustive manner in the FSR, e.g. offering access to infrastructure or essential facilities that were acquired or supported by the foreign subsidies; reducing capacity or market presence; refraining from certain investments; licensing of assets acquired with the help of foreign subsidies; the divestment of certain assets; requiring the undertakings to dissolve the concentration[301] concerned; the repayment of the foreign subsidy; and requiring the undertakings concerned to adapt their governance structure.[302]

The FSR sets forth three instruments (also referred to as "modules"[303]) to be used by the EU Commission in proceedings dealing with foreign subsidies. The first module is of general application and empowers the Commission to *ex officio* review foreign subsidies. If the Commission, on the basis of a preliminary review, has indications that an undertaking has received a foreign subsidy that distorts the Internal Market, it is required to start an in-depth investigation during which it may adopt interim measures, request information from undertakings under investigation as well as from Member States and third countries.[304] Moreover, it may conduct inspections within and outside the Union. Where an undertaking that receives, or a third country that granted, a foreign subsidy does not sufficiently cooperate, the Commission may take decisions on the basis of the facts available. In addition, it is empowered to impose fines and periodic penalty payments where an undertaking fails to comply with its procedural obligations under the FSR or a Commission decision imposing redressive measures.[305]

"Module 2" is concerned with concentrations, which are deemed to arise where a lasting change of control results from a merger, acquisition or joint venture as

---

298 Art. 4 of the FSR.

299 Art. 5 of the FSR.

300 Art. 6 of the FSR.

301 On the notion of concentrations cf in the following text.

302 Art. 7(4) of the FSR.

303 EU Commission, White Paper on levelling the playing field as regards foreign subsidies, 17 June 2020, COM(2020)253 final, pp. 13 ff.

304 Art. 13 of the FSR.

305 Arts. 14-17 of the FSR.

defined in the FSR.[306] Concentrations in this sense must be notified to the Commission prior to their implementation.[307] The Commission is empowered to *inter alia* prohibit a concentration and to also impose fines or periodic penalty payments as under "Module 1".[308] Similar powers are vested in the Commission under "Module 3" which applies to foreign subsidies that risk causing distortions in public procurement procedures.[309]

Finally, Art. 44(9) of the FSR refers to WTO law, stressing in particular that "no action shall be taken under this Regulation which would amount to a specific action against a subsidy within the meaning of Art. 32.1 of the Agreement on Subsidies and Countervailing Measures". However, this clause arguably does not sufficiently prevent conflicts with WTO law, in particular in view of the fact that the EU Commission seems to assume that the ASCM does not apply to foreign subsidies as just defined.[310]

4.3.3 WTO Disciplines Relevant for Foreign Subsidies

4.3.3.1 Pertinent ASCM Obligations

The WTO disciplines that are primarily relevant for subsidies relating to trade in goods have been laid down in the Agreement on Subsidies and Countervailing Measures (ASCM), which elaborates on the disciplines on subsidies contained in the GATT (Arts. VI and XVI of the latter). According to the definition set forth in Art. 1.1 ASCM, a subsidy is deemed to exist if:

> (a)(1) there is a financial contribution by a government or any public body within the territory of a Member (referred to in this Agreement as 'government') [...] or
> (a)(2) there is any form of income or price support in the sense of Art. XVI of GATT 1994 and
> (b) a benefit is thereby conferred.

Art. 1.2 ASCM goes on to provide that:

> [a] subsidy as defined in paragraph 1 shall be subject to the provisions of Part II or shall be subject to the provisions of Part III or V only if such a subsidy is specific in accordance with the provisions of Art. 2.

306 Art. 20(1) refers to (a) "the merger of two or more previously independent undertakings or parts of undertakings"; and (b) "the acquisition, by one or more persons already controlling at least one undertaking, or by one or more undertakings, whether by purchase of securities or assets, by contract or by any other means, of direct or indirect control of the whole or parts of one or more other undertakings". Art. 20(2) refers to "[t]he creation of a joint venture performing on a lasting basis all the functions of an autonomous economic entity".

307 Arts. 21 and 24 of the FSR.

308 Arts. 25-26 of the FSR.

309 Arts. 27 ff of the FSR.

310 On this cf als Tokas (2022), pp.781; Frank (2023), pp. 946 ff.

Part II, which is referenced in the latter provision, deals with so-called prohibited subsidies (namely export subsidies and import substitution subsidies) and sets out the multilateral remedies (i.e. WTO dispute settlement proceedings) available to challenge such subsidies. Part III is concerned with so-called actionable subsidies and the multilateral remedies that can be used to contest this type of subsidies; such a challenge is possible, if a subsidy of this type causes "adverse effects to the interests of another Member".[311] In the alternative, Part V enables WTO Members to unilaterally offset prohibited and actionable subsidies through the application of countervailing duties.[312]

Importantly, according to Art. 1.2 ASCM, such multilateral and unilateral measures are only available, if the subsidy at issue is specific as defined in Art. 2 ASCM. Pursuant to Art. 2.1 ASCM, a subsidy must be "specific to an enterprise or industry or group of enterprises or industries (referred to in this Agreement as 'certain enterprises') within the jurisdiction of the granting authority". By contrast, prohibited subsidies are *per se* deemed to be specific by virtue of Art. 2.3 ASCM. It is also relevant for the context of foreign services that Art. 25.2 requires WTO Members to notify subsidies as defined in Art. 1.1 ASCM that are "granted or maintained within their territories". It is to be noted, furthermore, that Art. 32.1 ASCM sets forth a *numerus clausus* principle by providing that "[n]o specific action against a subsidy of another Member can be taken except in accordance with the provisions of GATT 1994, as interpreted by [the ASCM]".

4.3.3.2 Pertinent GATS Obligations

As indicated above, the GATS does not lay down disciplines governing subsidies granted *for* services or investment. However, the GATS may indeed apply to *measures taken against* subsidies, to the extent that such measures affect trade in services including in particular foreign service suppliers (i.e. investors) that have established a commercial presence in the sense of Art. 1.2(c) of the GATS in the Member resorting to such measures.[313] In this regard, the most-favoured-nation-treatment clause (Art. II of GATS) and the national treatment requirement (Art. XVII of the GATS), which have been discussed already above,[314] are of particular relevance as will be seen in the following.

[311] Cf. Art. 5 of the ASCM.

[312] Cf. Art. VI of GATT 1994, Art. 10 and the definition of countervailing duties in footnote 36 of the ASCM, respectively.

[313] Cf. e.g. Herrmann and Ellemann (2024), p. 80; Ru and Yiqian (2022), pp. 67 ff.

[314] Cf. above, Sect. 4.1.3.2.

4.3.3.3 Potential Violations of the ASCM and the GATS

The FSR Assessed Under the ASCM

In order to determine whether the FSR violates the EU's obligations under the ASCM, it is necessary to analyse two issues:

- First, does the scope of the ASCM cover foreign subsidies?
- Second, does the FSR violate the ASCM in that it enables the EU to take unilateral measures that may be excluded by the *numerus clausus* principle enshrined in Art. 32.1 of the ASCM?

Regarding the first issue, it is to be noted that the ASCM does not explicitly address foreign subsidies.[315] As indicated above, the WTO Expert Group on Trade Financing has found that it is "not entirely clear whether or not the [ASCM] applies where the subsidizing entity is not within the territory of the Member whose goods are allegedly being subsidized".[316] This issue has not so far been clarified in WTO dispute settlement either.[317] It is necessary, therefore, to interpret relevant provisions in the ASCM, starting with the definition of "subsidies" in Art. 1.1 of the ASCM. As noted above, according to this provision a subsidy is deemed to exist if "there is a financial contribution by a government or any public body within the territory of *a* Member (referred to in this Agreement as 'government') [...] and a benefit is thereby conferred".

As regards the wording of this definition, it is conspicuous that it refers to financial contributions that are granted by "*a* Member" of the WTO, but not to "*the* Member" where the recipient of the contribution or the benefit is located; the same holds true for the French and Spanish versions of the ASCM.[318] Furthermore, as noted by *Crochet* and *Hegde* as well as *Crochet* and *Gustafsson*, the qualifier term "*within the territory* of a Member" in this definition refers to the preceding term "government or any public body", but not to "financial contribution". Hence, the term "within the territory of a Member" arguably does not indicate where the recipient of the financial contribution must be located,[319] a reading which is also confirmed by the fact that "by a government or any public body" is not put between

[315] On this and the following cf. in particular the excellent analyses by Crochet and Gustafsson (2021), pp. 347 ff and Crochet and Hegde (2020), pp. 6 ff; see also the obviously concurring view of Herrmann and Ellemann (2024), pp. 74 ff; cf. also the partly concurring view of Nagy (2023), pp. 890 ff; and Frank (2023), pp. 938 ff.

[316] Cf. WTO General Council, Working Group on Trade, Debt and Finance. WTO document WT/GC/W/527, WT/WGTDF/W/22, 16 March 2004; on this see also Crochet and Hegde (2020), pp. 1 ff; Gam and Papaefthymiou (2023) pp. 4 ff.

[317] See also Frank (2023), pp. 938 ff.

[318] This is also pointed out by Frank (2023), pp. 938 ff, who refers to the French and Spanish versions of this clause ("du resort territorial d'*un* Membre"; "en el territorio de *un* Miembro"; italics added).

[319] See also Frank (2023), pp. 938 ff.

commas.[320] It should also be noted that the parties in the *US–FSC* and *Brazil–Aircraft* disputes agreed that the recipient of the financial contribution need not be in the territory of the WTO Member granting the financial contribution.[321] It can therefore be concluded that financial contributions that are granted to recipients located outside the territory of the subsidizing Member are not excluded from the definition of subsidies. Furthermore, the wording "a benefit is thereby conferred" does not require that the recipient of the "benefit"[322] is located in the territory of the subsidizing Member. Hence, subsidies that benefit a recipient located outside of the territory of the subsidizing Member do not seem to be excluded from the ASCM definition of subsidies either.[323] Therefore, foreign subsidies can arguably be regarded as coming under the definition of subsidies set out in the ASCM and, therefore, under the scope of the ASCM.[324]

Importantly, however, the location of the recipient of the *benefit* determines whether the *remedies* defined in the ASCM are available (as clarified in WTO dispute settlement, the relevant recipient of the benefit is the producer of the products at issue[325]). This is where Arts. 1.2 and 2 of the ASCM come into play. As mentioned earlier, pursuant to Art. 1.2, the multilateral and unilateral remedies set forth in Parts II, III and V of the ASCM are only available, if a subsidy is "specific" as defined in more detail in Art. 2 of the ASCM.

As indicated above, Art. 2.3 makes it clear that prohibited subsidies—i.e. export subsidies and import substitution subsidies—are *ex lege* deemed to be specific. This implies that foreign export subsidies and foreign substitution subsidies could, in principle, be challenged in the multilateral WTO dispute settlement proceedings provided for in Part II of the ASCM. As has been argued in the literature, it is, however, quite unlikely that a WTO Member will contest foreign *export* subsidies that are granted to recipients located in its territory, given that such subsidies will usually benefit that WTO Member. On the other hand, it appears rather unrealistic from an economic point of view that a WTO Member will grant foreign *import substitution* subsidies, as this would usually benefit other WTO Members but not itself.[326]

---

[320] Crochet and Hegde (2020), p. 6; Crochet and Gustafsson (2021), p. 348.

[321] Crochet and Hegde (2020), p. 6; Frank (2023), pp. 938 ff.

[322] As emphasized by Crochet and Hegde (2020), pp. 8 ff, one needs to draw a distinction between the recipient of a given financial contribution and the recipient of the benefits actually arising from the financial contribution: thus, in the example of an export buyer credit, the recipient of the financial contribution will be the buyer who is located abroad. The recipients of the "benefit" accruing from this financial contribution may however be both the foreign buyer and the (domestic) producer who exports the products in question.

[323] Crochet and Gustafsson (2021), p. 348.

[324] See also Nagy (2023) 890 ff; Herrmann and Ellemann (2024), pp. 74 ff.

[325] Cf. Crochet and Gustafsson (2021), pp. 348–349 with further references to WTO dispute settlement reports.

[326] Cf. Crochet and Gustafsson (2021), pp. 350–351.

As regards other subsidies—i.e. subsidies that are not per se prohibited, but potentially *actionable* under the ASCM[327]—the availability of the multilateral remedies set out in Part III hinges on the definition of "specificity" in Art. 2 of the ASCM. Crucially, in order for an actionable subsidy to be specific in this sense, it must be specific to enterprises "*within the jurisdiction* of the granting authority".[328] As pointed out in academic writings, "jurisdiction" in this clause should evidently be interpreted as referring to the subsidizing Member's *territory*. This follows in particular from the legislative history of the ASCM, given that the originally proposed wording of this provision has been changed from "territory" to "jurisdiction" merely to accommodate Canadian concerns that subsidies offered by Canadian provinces could be deemed to be specific even if they were generally applicable in a given Canadian province. This reading is also confirmed by Art. 25.2 and footnote 63 to paragraph 2 of Annex IV of the ASCM, which both refer to the subsidizing Member's territory.[329] Furthermore, the WTO Appellate Body and the US in the *US–FSC* proceedings have interpreted "jurisdiction" as referring to a Member's territory.[330] In the light of this interpretation of the wording "*within the jurisdiction* of the granting authority", actionable foreign subsidies arguably cannot be regarded as specific. Consequently, the *multilateral* DSU proceedings provided for in Part III of the ASCM do not seem available for this type of foreign subsidies.[331]

This interim conclusion leads to the *second of the aforementioned issues*, namely the question as to whether it is permissible under the ASCM for the EU to have resort to the *unilateral* measures laid down in its FSR, such as redressive measures and fines. The ASCM regulates unilateral measures in Part V. Such countervailing measures may take the form of countervailing duties (i.e. duties that are levied for the purpose of offsetting subsidies that are granted "directly or indirectly upon the manufacture, production or export of any merchandise"),[332] provisional measures[333] or price undertakings.[334] Crucially, countervailing duties are futile as regards foreign subsidies, as the subsidized producer of the products at issue is already within the country.[335]

Importantly, as noted above, pursuant to the *numerus clausus* principle enshrined in Art. 32.1 of the ASCM, "[n]o specific action against a subsidy of another Member can be taken except in accordance with the provisions of GATT 1994, as interpreted

---

327 On the concept of actionable subsidies see above, Sect. 4.3.3.1.

328 Art. 2.1 of the ASCM.

329 Crochet and Hegde (2020), p. 13.

330 Cf. Crochet and Gustafsson (2021), p. 350, referring to the proceedings in *US–Shrimp* (Appellate Body Report, *United States – Shrimp*, WT/DS58/AB/R, adopted 6 November 1998, DSR 1998:VII, p. 2755, para 133) and *US–FSC* (WTO Panel Report, *United States – Tax Treatment for 'Foreign Sales Corporations'* (Art. 21.5 DSU), WT/DS/108/R, 8 October 1999, at Annex F-3, para 108.

331 Cf. Crochet and Gustafsson (2021), p. 350; see also Crochet and Hegde (2020), pp. 6 ff.

332 Cf. Art. 10 and footnote 36 of the ASCM.

333 Cf. Art. 17 of the ASCM.

334 Cf. Art. 18 of the ASCM.

335 Cf. Crochet and Gustafsson (2021), pp. 351–352.

by [the ASCM]". Hence, the answer to the question as to whether the EU may impose the unilateral measures provided for in the FSR, such as redressive measures and fines, depends on the interpretation of Art. 32.1 of the ASCM.[336] As emphasized in WTO dispute settlement, the two central criteria in the wording of Art. 32.1 are "specific to subsidization" and "taken [...] against subsidization". A unilateral measure has been regarded by the Appellate Body as being "specific to subsidization", if it is "inextricably linked to" or has a "strong correlation with the constituent elements" of a subsidy.[337] Furthermore, a unilateral measure is understood as being taken "against subsidization", when its "design and structure [...] is such that the measure is 'opposed to', has an adverse bearing on, or, more specifically, has the effect of dissuading [...] the practice of subsidization, or creates an incentive to terminate such practices".[338] As has been argued in the literature, the unilateral redressive measures and fines set forth in the FSR clearly fulfill these criteria, as they are evidently linked to foreign subsidies and may have the effect of "dissuading" or "terminating" foreign subsidies.[339] This seems to imply that a measure such as the FSR infringes the *numerus clausus* principle in Art. 32.1 of the ASCM.

However, as argued by *Crochet* and *Gustafsson*, this reading of Art. 32.1 has the consequence that WTO Members would not be allowed to take measures against challenges posed by foreign subsidies that had not been foreseen by the drafters of the ASCM.[340] *Crochet* and *Gustafsson* therefore point to two alternative interpretations: First, a panel might read the ASCM as not covering foreign subsidies, which would incur the consequence that unilateral measures against such subsidies would not be prohibited.[341] Since this would arguably go against the spirit of the ASCM, *Crochet* and *Gustafsson* argue that unilateral measures such as those envisaged in the EU's FSR should be regarded as falling under Art. 32.1 of the ASCM on the basis of the reasons discussed before, but that one should consider whether the *prima facie* violation of the ASCM could possibly be justified under the general exceptions clause of the GATT, i.e. Art. XX. We will come back to this issue in Sect. 4.3.3.4.

---

336 On this and the following see again Crochet and Gustafsson (2021), pp. 352 ff; see also Tokas (2022), pp. 794 ff.

337 Cf. the Appellate Body Report, *US — Offset Act (Byrd Amendment)*, (WT/DS217/AB/R, WT/DS234/AB/R) para 239.

338 Cf. the Appellate Body Report, *US — Offset Act (Byrd Amendment)*, (WT/DS217/AB/R, WT/DS234/AB/R) para 256.

339 Crochet and Gustafsson (2021), p. 354; see also Tokas (2022), pp. 794 ff.

340 Crochet and Gustafsson (2021), p. 354.

341 This view is actually taken in the literature by Nagy (2023), pp. 889 ff.

The FSR Assessed Under the GATS

As previously indicated, aside from the hortatory disciplines set out in Art. XV, the GATS does not contain rules on subsidies for services and investments. For this reason, it has been submitted that the application of the FSR to subsidies and investments does not pose any concerns under WTO law.[342] However, this is a questionable conclusion, since it has to be recalled that the GATS applies to any "measures by Members affecting trade in services". Moreover, as mentioned above, trade in services covers the "commercial presence" of foreign service suppliers according to Art. I.2(c) of the GATS.[343] Therefore, the GATS is patently relevant for unilateral measures which are taken *against* services and investments.[344] Consequently, there is a palpable risk that the unilateral measures provided for in the EU FSR could contravene central GATS principles, namely its most-favoured-nation (MFN) and national treatment (NT) clauses, i.e. Arts. II and XVII, respectively.

First, as regards the MFN clause, to the extent that suppliers of services of different WTO Members may have to be regarded as like service suppliers[345] irrespective of whether they receive foreign subsidies, the question arises as to whether such suppliers are subject to differential treatment under the FSR. Given that the FSR targets foreign subsidies independently from the nationality of the undertakings receiving such subsidies, the FSR is not *de jure* discriminatory in the sense of the MFN clause in this respect.[346] However, there is a risk that the application of the FSR by the EU Commission could incur negative asymmetric impacts for undertakings of certain WTO Members, in particular China.[347] In this regard, it has been pointed out in the literature that the FSR has been adopted in especially to target foreign subsidies granted by China and Chinese undertakings.[348] While it has rightly been argued that the question of whether such discriminatory effects will *de facto* materialize depends on how the EU Commission uses the discretion granted to it under the FSR,[349] it has indeed been observed that the clear majority of cases examined by the EU Commission so far have concerned China.[350]

Second, as respects the national treatment (NT) clause, the application of the FSR likewise raises the spectre of *de facto* discrimination.[351] This is due in especially to the procedural rules under the FSR, which diverge considerably from the

---

[342] Frank (2023), p. 939.

[343] On this see already above, Sect. 4.1.3.2.

[344] Crochet and Gustafsson (2021), pp. 356 ff; Herrmann and Ellemann (2024), p. 80.

[345] On the notion of likeness in the GATS context cf above, Sect. 4.1.3.2.

[346] See also Crochet and Gustafsson (2021), pp. 356 ff; Herrmann and Ellemann (2024), p. 81.

[347] Crochet and Gustafsson (2021), pp. 356 ff.

[348] See e.g. Ding Ru and Yiquian (2022), pp. 68 ff.

[349] Herrmann and Ellemann (2024), p. 81.

[350] Cf. Cleary Gottlieb (2024); on this see already above, Sect. 4.3.3.3.2.

[351] See also Ding Ru and Yiqian (2022), pp. 68 ff.

disciplines applicable to undertakings under EU state aid law.[352] This holds true e.g. for the different administrative burdens for undertakings arising under EU state aid law on the one hand and the FSR on the other hand, as well as for the divergent procedural deadlines (which tend to be stricter under the FSR), different procedural rights and remedies, and deviating requirements to repay subsidies.[353] Not all of these divergences will necessarily have negative asymmetric impacts for undertakings receiving foreign services, however.[354] Hence, whether discriminatory effects arise in the application of the FSR will depend, under the NT clause as well, on how the EU Commission exercises its discretion under this Regulation.[355]

Of course, whether and to what extent the GATS NT clause is relevant for the FSR depends on whether the EU has undertaken pertinent commitments in its GATS schedule as well as on whether it has scheduled exemptions for subsidies.[356] First, regarding the issue of exemptions, while the EU has scheduled a horizontal exemption relating to subsidies "for branches established in a Member State by a non-Community company", this exemption does not apply to several Member States.[357] Second, as regards "services incidental to energy distribution", the EU has not undertaken commitments under the NT clause; however, Hungary, Latvia, Lithuania and Slovenia have arguably entered into full commitments in this respect.[358] In this respect, it should additionally be recalled that a WTO Member's regulations can be challenged, whenever services or services suppliers are affected in *any* services sector for which a WTO Member has undertaken commitments. Hence, the EU FSR does not seem to be fully immunized from challenges under the GATS.

4.3.3.4 Justification of Violations of WTO Law

As discussed in previous chapters already, *prima facie* violations of the GATT and the GATS can in principle be justified under the general exceptions clauses of the GATT and GATS (Art. XX of the GATT and Art. XIV of the GATS, respectively).[359] Moreover, the security exceptions of both agreements (Art. XXI of the GATT and Art. XIV*bis* of the GATS) can become relevant, given that the latter could in particular be invoked in situations concerning energy security.[360]

However, as regards the ASCM, the question arises whether Art. XX of the GATT could be relied upon in an attempt to justify violations of the ASCM, *in*

[352] Cf. also Herrmann and Ellemann (2024), p. 80 ff.

[353] Cf. Nagy (2023), p. 906.

[354] Cf. Nagy (2023), p. 906.

[355] Cf. also Herrmann and Ellemann (2024), p. 81.

[356] On the functioning of GATS schedules cf Van den Bossche and Zdouc (2022), pp. 571 ff.

[357] Cf. the GATS Schedule of the EU, WTO document GATS/SC/157, 7 May 2019, p. 6.

[358] Cf. the GATS Schedule of the EU, WTO document GATS/SC/157, 7 May 2019, p. 83.

[359] Cf. above, Sects. 4.1.3.4 and 4.2.3.5.

[360] Cf. above, Sect. 4.1.3.4.2.

concreto Art. 32.1 of the ASCM. An analogous question arises regarding the relationship between the ASCM and Art. XXI of the GATT. With respect to the relationship between Art. 32.1 of the ASCM and Art. XX of the GATT, it has been argued in the literature that Art. XX cannot be invoked to justify subsidies that violate the ASCM.[361] However, it has been stressed that the question to be examined is not the relationship between Art. XX of the GATT and another agreement such as the ASCM as a whole, but the specific relationship between Art. XX and a concrete provision like Art. 32.1 of the ASCM.[362] In this context, it appears also relevant that footnote 56 to Art. 32.1 stipulates that this provision "is not intended to preclude action under other relevant provisions of GATT 1994, where appropriate". On this basis, *Crochet* and *Gustafsson* have convincingly submitted that Art. XX could arguably be invoked to justify a violation of Art. 32.1 of the ASCM, a conclusion which seems to be confirmed also by the legislative history and the objects and purpose of the ASCM.[363] Furthermore, on the ground that one needs to assess the relationship between a concrete exceptions clause laid down in the GATT and *concrete* provisions of other WTO agreements, one can arguably similarly submit that it may be possible to invoke the security exceptions clause enshrined in Art. XXI of the GATT to justify infringements of Art. 32.1 of the ASCM.[364]

With respect to the general exceptions clauses in the GATT and the GATS, it has been submitted that the EU could possibly rely in Art. XX(d) of the GATT, which has already been examined above,[365] and the analogous provision of Art. XIV(c) of the GATS in order to defend the FSR.[366] Both provisions make it possible for WTO Members to justify measures that are "necessary to secure compliance with laws or regulations which are not inconsistent with the provisions" of the respective agreements. Hence, the EU could refer to the existence of its internal state aid regime, arguing that it requires to be complemented by a regime on foreign subsidies.[367] As has been explained previously, WTO panels have traditionally applied considerable deference when WTO Members argue that they pursue any of the policy goals mentioned in Art. XX of the GATT or Art. XIV of the GATS.[368]

Furthermore, the EU could try to invoke Art. XX(a) of the GATT and Art. XIV(a) of the GATS in order to justify the FSR. Pursuant to Art. XX(a) of the GATT, a WTO Member may take measures that are "necessary to protect public morals". Art. XIV(a) of the GATS, on the other hand, makes it possible to adopt measures that are "necessary to protect public morals or to maintain public order". As

[361] Cf. Crochet and Gustafsson (2021), p. 355, with further references.

[362] Cf. Crochet and Gustafsson (2021), p. 355, with further references.

[363] Cf. Crochet and Gustafsson (2021), p. 355 with further references.

[364] For space restraints, the following analysis will concentrate on the general exceptions clauses of the GATT and the GATS (i.e. Art. XX of the GATT and Art. XIV of the GATS). On the functioning and application of the security exceptions in the energy context, cf. already above in Sect. 4.1.3.4.2.

[365] Cf. above, Sect. 4.2.3.5.3.

[366] Cf. Crochet and Gustafsson (2021), pp. 359 ff; Nagy (2023), pp. 906–907.

[367] Cf. Crochet and Gustafsson (2021), pp. 359 ff; Nagy (2023), pp. 906–907.

[368] Cf. above, Sect. 4.2.3.5.1; see also Crochet and Gustafsson (2021), pp. 359 ff.

emphasized by *Crochet* and *Gustafsson*, WTO panel practice has confirmed that the ground of "public order" can in principle be invoked to justify measures preventing unfair competition.[369] Moreover, to the extent that the FSR is employed to protect the *Internal Energy Market*, it should be recalled that WTO dispute settlement practice has accepted that energy security is covered by the notion of "public order" in Art. XIV(a) of the GATS.[370]

Crucially, Arts. XX(a) and XX(d) of the GATT as well as Arts. XIV(a) and XIV(c) of the GATS require an analysis as to whether a measure such as the FSR is actually "necessary" for the legitimate objectives set forth in these provisions. In this context, it has been submitted that the considerable procedural burden under the FSR may be problematic under the necessity test, as milder and more suitable means may be available, such as an approach in which investigations are only triggered in circumstances in which an undertaking's conduct deviates from normal market behaviour.[371] However, as highlighted earlier, the "weighing and balancing approach" adopted by the WTO Appellate Body within the necessity test—which takes into account in particular a measure's contribution to a legitimate policy objective, the importance of this objective, and the degree of a measure's trade effect[372]—may allow for justification under the necessity criterion, in particular in situations related to energy security, which has been found in panel practice to be of "fundamental importance" and therefore of particular weight.[373]

As stated in previous chapters already, if a measure can be regarded as being provisionally justified under one of the paragraphs of Art. XX of the GATT or Art. XIV of the GATS, it must also be demonstrated that such a measure is in line with the analogous Chapeaus of these provisions. These require that a trade measure is not "applied in a manner which would constitute a means of arbitrary or unjustifiable discrimination between countries where the same conditions prevail, or a disguised restriction" on international trade in goods or services. As stated above,[374] the common theme of these criteria is that of "avoiding abuse or illegitimate use" of the general exceptions clauses,[375] which in particular implies that a WTO Member must not "require other Members to adopt essentially the same comprehensive program [...] without taking into considerations different conditions which may occur in the territories of those other Members".[376] Discrimination can be found to be "arbitrary and unjustifiable" in especially "when the application of the measure at issue does not allow for any inquiry into the appropriateness of the regulatory program for the

---

369 Crochet and Gustafsson (2021), p. 360.

370 Cf. above, Sect. 4.1.3.4.1.

371 Crochet and Gustafsson (2021), pp. 360–361.

372 Cf. above, Sect. 4.1.3.4.1.

373 Cf. above, Sect. 4.1.3.4.1.

374 Cf. above, Sect. 4.2.3.5.6.

375 Appellate Body Report, *United States – Gasoline*, p. 22.

376 Appellate Body Report, *United States – Shrimp*, para 164.

conditions prevailing in those exporting countries".[377] Moreover, as previously explained, such arbitrary discrimination arises in particular, when a WTO Member "imposes a single, rigid and unbending requirement" for other Members to adopt essentially the same program as its own.[378] According to the Appellate Body, WTO Members ought to recognize foreign programs that are "comparable in effectiveness".[379] Furthermore, the Appellate Body has held that discrimination may be found to be "unjustifiable" when the discriminatory effects were foreseeable and were "not merely inadvertent or unavoidable".[380] Additionally, the Appellate Body has found that an importing Member is required "to engage [...] in serious, across-the-board negotiations" before imposing unilateral trade-restrictive measures.[381]

In the light of these guidelines, it has been argued that the FSR may contravene the Chapeaus of Art. XX of the GATT and Art. XIV of the GATS both in substantive and procedural terms. In terms of the FSR's substantive requirements, it is in particular conspicuous that the FSR does not replicate the exceptions that are recognized in Art. 107 TFEU; moreover, it provides for redressive measures that are more incisive than those applicable under EU state aid law.[382] With regard to procedural differences, it has been noted that undertakings may face significantly heavier burdens under the FSR than under EU state aid law.[383] Further, it has been argued that the significant investigatory and redressive powers vested in the EU Commission under the FSR that are paired with wide margins of discretion risk resulting in arbitrary discrimination.[384] On the other hand, however, it is this margin of discretion which could also be used by the Commission to avoid applying the FSR in an arbitrary manner.[385] It is problematic, however, that the Commission reportedly has not engaged in "serious, across-the-board negotations", as required in Appellate Body dispute settlement practice,[386] before imposing its unilateral FSR.[387] Moreover, this device could be regarded – paraphrasing the Appellate Body—as a "single, rigid and unbending requirement",[388] which could be regarded as being too inflexible to take into account equivalent regimes existing in other WTO Members.[389]

For these reasons, it cannot be ruled out that the FSR may be found to violate WTO law.

---

[377] Appellate Body Report, *United States – Shrimp*, para 165.

[378] Appellate Body Report, *United States – Shrimp*, para 177.

[379] Appellate Body Report, *United States – Shrimp*, para 144.

[380] Appellate Body Report, *United States – Gasoline*, pp. 28 ff.

[381] Appellate Body Report, *United States – Shrimp*, para 166.

[382] Crochet and Gustafsson (2021), pp. 361 ff; see also Herrmann and Ellemann (2024), pp. 74 ff.

[383] Crochet and Gustafsson (2021), pp. 361 ff; see also Nagy (2023), pp. 905 ff.

[384] Crochet and Gustafsson (2021), p. 362.

[385] Herrmann and Ellemann (2024), p. 81.

[386] Appellate Body Report, *United States – Shrimp*, para 166.

[387] Crochet and Gustafsson (2021), pp. 361 ff; Frank (2023), p. 926.

[388] Appellate Body Report, *United States – Shrimp*, para 177. On this see also already above, Sect. 4.2.3.5.6.

[389] Crochet and Gustafsson (2021), p. 363.

References

Bacchus J (2021) Legal Issues with the European Carbon Border Adjustment Mechanism. Cato Institute Briefing Paper No. 125. https://www.cato.org/briefing-paper/legal-issues-european-carbon-border-adjustment-mechanism#

Bauerle Danzman S, Meunier S (2021) The Big Screen: Mapping the Diffusion of Foreign Investment Screening Mechanisms, 27 September 2021, available via SSRN, https://papers.ssrn.com/sol3/papers.cfm?abstract_id=3913248

Bohnert S (2022) EU investment screening: a roadblock in a one-way street? In: Winner M (ed) Kontrolle ausländischer Direktinvestitionen in Mittel- und Osteuropa. Facultas, Vienna, pp 9–97

Charnovitz S (2002) The law of environmental 'PPMs' in the WTO: debunking the myth of illegality. Yale J Int Law 27:59–110

Cheng B (2021) Foreign direct investment screening and national security. J World Investment Trade 22:561–595

Choukroune L, Nedumpara JJ (2021) International economic law. Cambridge University Press, Cambridge, UK

Cleary Gottlieb (2024) The EU Foreign Subsidies Regulation in Practice: First Cases and Enforcement Trends, 11 June 2024, Available at https://www.clearygottlieb.com/news-and-insights/publication-listing/the-eu-foreign-subsidies-regulation-in-practice-first-cases-and-enforcement-trends.

Cottier T, Shariff N (2013) International trade and climate change. In: Van Calster G, Prévost D (eds) Research handbook on environment, health and the WTO. Edward Elgar, Cheltenham, UK, pp 413–447

Crochet V, Gustafsson M (2021) Lawful remedy or illegal response? Resolving the issue of foreign subsidization under WTO law. World Trade Rev 20(3):343–366

Crochet V, Hegde V (2020) China's 'Going Global' policy: transnational production subsidies under the WTO SCM agreement. J Int Econ Law 00:1–23

Daly M (2005) The WTO and Direct Taxation. WTO Discussion Paper 9 (2005). https://www.wto.org/english/res_e/booksp_e/discussion_papers9_e.pdf

Delimatsis P (2006) Don't Gamble with GATS – the interaction between Articles VI, XVI, XVII and XVIII GATS in the Light of the US-Gambling Case. J World Trade 40(6):1059

Delimatsis P (2007) Due process and 'Good' regulation embedded in the GATS. J Int Econ Law 10(1):13–50

Demaret P, Stewardson R (1994) Border tax adjustments under GATT and EC law and general implications for environmental taxes. J World Trade 28(4):5–65

Dimitropoulos G (1999) National security: the role of investment screening mechanisms. https://ssrn.com/abstract=3538735

Dobson NL (2022) (Re)framing responsibility? Assessing the division of burdens under the EU Carbon border adjustment mechanism. Utrecht Law Rev 18(2):162–179

Eberhard H et al (2021) Europäisches und öffentliches Wirtschaftsrecht, vol 2, 11th edn. Verlag Österreich, Vienna

Ehring L (2002) De facto discrimination in world trade law. National and most-favoured-nation treatment–or equal treatment? J World Trade 36(5):921–977

Eichenberg MB (2010) Greenhouse gas regulation and border tax adjustments: the carrot and the stick. Golden Gate Univ Environ Law J 3(2/3):283–364

Englisch J, Falcao T (2021) EU Carbon Border Adjustments. Environmental Law Reporter 10-2021:10857–10858

Erixon F (2022) The new wave of defensive trade policy measures in the European Union: design, structure, and trade effects. ECIPE OCCASIONAL PAPER 04/2022. https://ecipe.org/wp-content/uploads/2022/05/ECI_22_OccPaper_Defence_04_2022_LY10.pdf

Espa I, Francois J, van Asselt H (2022) The EU proposal for a carbon border adjustment mechanism (CBAM): An Analysis under WTO and Climate Change Law. WTI working paper no. 06/2022.

https://www.wti.org/media/filer_public/ee/61/ee6171fd-a68d-4829-875e-d9b0c32298b5/wti_working_paper_06_2022.pdf
Fassion J, Natens B (2020) The EU proposal for FDI control: The WTO on the sidelines? In: Bourgeois JHJ (ed) EU framework for foreign direct investment control. Wolters Kluwer, Alphen an den Rijn, pp 121–134
Frank M (2023) The EU's new foreign subsidies regulation on collision course with the WTO. Common Mark Law Rev 60:925–958
Gam L, Papaefthymiou A (2023) The EU Foreign Subsidies Regulation. CPI Antitrust Chronicle 2023. https://www.competitionpolicyinternational.com/wp-content/uploads/2023/05/5-THE-EU-FOREIGN-SUBSIDIES-REGULATION-GREEN-SUBSIDIES-TREADING-THE-LINE-BETWEEN-THE-FSR-STATE-AID-AND-WTO-LAW-Liliane-Gam-Argyrios-Papaefthymiou.pdf
Hancher L, de Hauteclocque A (2024) Strategic autonomy, REPowerEU and the internal energy market: untying the Gordian Knot. Common Mark Law Rev 61(1):55–92
Herrmann C (2019) Europarechtliche Fragen der deutschen Investitionskontrolle. Zeitschrift für europarechtliche Studien 2019(3):429–476
Herrmann C, Ellemann T (2024) Die neue Verordnung über den Binnenmarkt verzerrende drittstaatliche Subventionen – Ein Brussels Effect in Zeiten geoökonomischer Subventionswettläufe? Zeitschrift für europäisches Privatrecht 32(1):64–104
Hillman JA (2013) Changing climate for carbon taxes: who's afraid of the WTO? Georgetown Climate & Energy Policy Paper Series, July 2013. https://scholarship.law.georgetown.edu/cgi/viewcontent.cgi?article=3048&context=facpub
Hollaus B, Mayr S (2022) Der CO2-Grenzausgleichsmechanismus der Europäischen Union: eine Klimaschutzmaßnahme und ihre WTO-rechtlichen Fallstricke. Österreichische Zeitschrift für Wirtschaftsrecht 102(3):102–114
Holzer K (2010) Proposals on Carbon-related border adjustments: prospects for WTO compliance. Carbon Clim Law Rev 4(1):51–64
Holzer K, Espa I, Cottier T (2022), Annex I. The EU CBAM and WTO Law, 30 November 2022, https://www.bafu.admin.ch/dam/bafu/de/dokumente/klima/rechtsgutachten/rechtsgutachten-zur-einfuehrung-eines-co2-grenzausgleichsmechanismus-in-der-schweiz.pdf.download.pdf/Rechtsgutachten%20CBAM%2030.11.22.pdf
Holzer K, Shariff N (2013) The Inclusion of Border Carbon Adjustments in Preferential Trade Agreements: Policy Implications. Carbon & Climate Law Review 6:246-260
Howse R, Regan D (2000) The product/process distinction – an illusory basis for disciplining 'Unilateralism' in trade policy. Eur J Int Law 11(2):249–289
Jackson JH (1997) The world trading system. Law and policy of international economic relations. MIT Press, Cambridge
Kendall K (2012) Carbon taxes and the WTO: a carbon charge without trade concerns? Arizona J Int Comp Law 29(1):49–89
Krajewski M (2003) National regulation and trade liberalization in services. Kluwer, The Hague
Low P, Marceau G, Reinaud J (2012) The interface between the trade and climate change regimes: scoping the issues. J World Trade 46(3):485–544
Matsushita M, Schoenbaum TJ, Mavroidis PC (2006) The World Trade Organization, 2nd edn. Oxford University Press, Oxford, UK
Nagy CI (2023) The EU's new regime on foreign subsidies: has the time come for a paradigm-shift? J World Trade 57(6):889–908
O'Brien J (2009) The equity of levelling the playing field in the climate change context. J World Trade 43(5):1093–1114
Pauwelyn J (2003) Conflict of norms in public international law. How WTO law relates to other rules of international law. Cambridge University Press, Cambridge
Pauwelyn J (2005) Rien ne Va Plus? Distinguishing Domestic Regulation from Market Access in GATT and GATS. Duke Law School Legal Studies Research Paper Series, Research Paper No. 85, October 2005, 131. http://papers.ssrn.com/sol3/papers.cfm?abstract_id=638303

Pauwelyn J (2012) Carbon leakage measures and border tax adjustments under WTO law. https://papers.ssrn.com/sol3/papers.cfm?abstract_id=2026879

Pauwelyn J, Kleimann D (2020) Trade related aspects of a carbon border adjustment mechanism. A legal assessment. Briefing 14-04-2020. https://www.europarl.europa.eu/thinktank/en/document/EXPO_BRI(2020)603502

Petersmann EU (1997) The GATT/WTO dispute settlement system: international law, international organizations and dispute settlement. Martinus Nijhoff Publishers, London

Pirlot A (2017) Environmental border tax adjustments and international trade law. Edward Elgar, Cheltenham

Pitschas C (2003) Allgemeines Übereinkommen über den Handel mit Dienstleistungen (GATS). In: Priess H-J et al (eds) WTO-Handbuch. C.H. Beck, Munich, pp 495–563

Puth S (2003) WTO und Umwelt. Die Produkt-Prozess-Doktrin. Duncker & Humblot, Berlin

Quick R (2020) Carbon border adjustment. A dissenting view on its alleged GATT-compatibility. Zeitschrift für europarechtliche Studien. Issue 4/2020:550–596

Rajavuori M, Huhta K (2020) Investment screening: implications for the energy sector and energy security. Energy Policy 144(2):111646. https://www.researchgate.net/publication/342491244_Investment_screening_Implications_for_the_energy_sector_and_energy_security

Raza W, Tröster B, Madner V, Mayr S, Hollaus B (2022) Analyse und Beurteilung des Vorschlags der Europäischen Kommission für einen CO2-Grenzausgleichsmechanismus (Carbon Border Adjustment Mechanism) der EU. https://www.oefse.at/publikationen/detail/publication/show/Publication/analyse-und-beurteilung-des-vorschlags-der-europaeischen-kommission-fuer-einen-co2-grenzausgleichsmechanismus-carbon-border-adjustment-mechanism-der-eu/

Ru D, Yiqian X (2022) Emerging rules on cross-border subsidies: A. typological analysis and proposals for China's approach. J WTO China 12(2):45–79

Ruddigkeit D (2009) Border Tax Adjustment an der Schnittstelle von Welthandelsrecht und Klimaschutz. Beiträge zum Transnationalen Wirtschaftsrecht, Heft 89. https://opendata.uni--halle.de/bitstream/1981185920/78533/1/BeitraegeTWR_89.pdf

Schill SW, Briese R (2009) "If the State Considers": self-judging clauses in international dispute settlement. In: von Bogdandy A, Wolfrum R (eds) Max Planck yearbook of United Nations Law 13:51–140

Tokas M (2022) Playing the game: the EU's proposed regulation on foreign subsidies. J World Trade 56(5):779–802

Trebilcock MJ, Howse R (1999) The regulation of international trade. Routledge, London, UK

Trüeb HR (2001) Umweltrecht in der WTO. Schulthess, Zurich, Switzerland

van Calster G (2000) International and EU trade law. The environmental challenge. Cameron May, London

Van den Bossche P, Zdouc W (2022) The law and policy of the World Trade Organization, 5th edn. Cambridge University Press, Cambridge

Velten J (2020) The Investment Screening Regulation and Its Screening Ground "Security or Public Order": How the WTO Law Understanding Undermines the Regulation's Objectives, https://repository.graduateinstitute.ch/record/298429?_ga=2.7440050.1223939625.1666604149-2031466909.1666604148&v=pdf

Voon T, Merriman D (2022) Incoming: how international investment law constrains foreign investment screening. JWIT 23(3):1–40

Vranes E (2003) The Banana dispute. fundamental issues in WTO law. In: Breuss F, Griller S, Vranes E (eds) The Banana dispute. An economic and legal analysis. Springer, Vienna/New York, pp 39–111

Vranes E (2009a) The overlap between GATT and GATS: a methodological maze. Leg Iss Econ Integr 36(3):215–238

Vranes E (2009b) The WTO and regulatory freedom: WTO disciplines on market access, non-discrimination and domestic regulation relating to trade in goods and services. J Int Econ Law 12(4):953–987

Vranes E (2009c) Trade and the environment. Fundamental issues in international law, WTO law and legal theory. Oxford University Press, Oxford

Vranes E (2009d) Climate change and the WTO. EU emission trading and the WTO disciplines on trade in goods, services and investment protection. J World Trade 43(4):707–735

Vranes E (2016) Carbon taxes, PPMs and the GATT. In: Delimatsis P (ed) Research handbook on climate change and trade law. Edward Elgar, Cheltenham, pp 77–108

Vranes E (2021) Environmental taxes and border tax adjustments. In: Delimatsis P, Reins L (eds) Trade and environmental law. Edward Elgar, Cheltenham, UK, pp 189–199

Vranes E (2023) Investment screening and WTO law: the example of the EU screening regulation. Springer Nature, Cham, Switzerland

Weiler JHH (2000) Epilogue: towards a common law of international trade. In: Weiler JHH (ed) The EU, the WTO, and the NAFTA. Towards a common law of international trade? Oxford University Press, Oxford, pp 201–232

Weiss W, Ohler C, Bungenberg M (2022) Welthandelsrecht, 3rd edn. C.H. Beck, Munich

Winter G (2001) Welthandelsrecht und Umweltschutz. In: Dolde KP (ed) Umweltrecht im Wandel. Erich Schmidt Verlag, Berlin, pp 71–98

Zdouc W (1999) WTO dispute settlement practice relating to the GATS. J Int Econ Law 2(2):295–346

Chapter 5
Conclusions

Abstract This study has examined the relationship between EU energy politics and WTO law, focusing on how the EU's Internal Energy Market can be promoted and protected through three crucial "horizontal" instruments (the EU Screening Regulation, the EU CBAM Mechanism and the EU Foreign Subsidies Regulation) in a way that is consistent with the requirements of WTO law. The results of this analysis are summarized in this Section. Overall, this study has shown that while it is strategically imperative to protect the EU Internal Energy Market from undue foreign influence in order to promote the EU's "strategic energy autonomy" and its "open strategic autonomy" more generally, it is not an easy task to promote this objective on the basis of unilateral measures such as those analysed in this treatise in a WTO-compliant manner.

This study has examined the relationship between EU energy politics and WTO law, focusing on how the EU's Internal Energy Market can be promoted and protected in a way that is consistent with the requirements of WTO law.

The necessity of a distinctive reorientation of the EU foreign policy, including its trade and energy policy, has become evident in the light of today's rapidly changing geopolitical context. Many states are reacting to this situation by seeking to increase their "strategic sovereignty". In the EU, this reorientation is taking place under the leitmotivs of "strategic autonomy" in its external affairs and "open strategic autonomy" in the EU's foreign trade context.[1]

Given that the many current geopolitical shifts also affect the international energy landscape, it has been argued that the EU must increase its "strategic *energy* autonomy".[2] This is seen as requiring the EU to adapt its energy policy both externally vis à vis third states and internally, within the Internal Energy Market, given that the EU's external energy dependence is directly connected to its internal energy

[1] Cf. above, Chap. 1.

[2] Hancher and de Hauteclocque (2024), p. 59.

E. Vranes, *EU Energy Politics and WTO Law*, SpringerBriefs in Law,
https://doi.org/10.1007/978-3-032-02392-6_5

policy and its approach to energy transition within the Internal Market.[3] Since the EU Internal Energy Market is thus perceived as being central to promoting the EU's energy autonomy, the Internal Energy Market needs to be protected from undue foreign influences. In this respect, three horizontal unilateral tools forming part of the EU's reorientation towards open strategic autonomy[4] are seen as essential: the EU Investment Screening Regulation, the EU Carbon Border Adjustment Mechanism (CBAM) and the EU Foreign Subsidies Regulation.[5]

The EU Investment Screening Regulation, as the first of these instruments, is crucial for helping to control the influx of third-country foreign direct investments into relevant EU industries and infrastructure. The second instrument, the CBAM, is considered requisite to prevent that EU undertakings falling under the EU Emission Trading System relocate to third countries. The Foreign Subsidies Regulation, as the third of these horizontal mechanisms, is seen as necessary to guarantee fair competition for EU companies subject to EU state aid rules vis à vis competitors that benefit from subsidies granted by third states.

This study has tried to clarify the extent to which these novel instruments and their application may contravene WTO law. First, as regards the **EU Investment Screening Regulation**, it has been shown that individual screening decisions could violate the most-favoured-nation (MFN) principles of the GATT and the GATS. Similarly, screening measures could e.g. infringe the national treatment clause of the GATT and central provisions of the GATS, such as Art. XVI (setting forth market access disciplines) and Art. XVII (requiring national treatment). Additionally, national implementing measures could e.g. violate the transparency standards of the GATT and the GATS. While *prima facie* violations of GATT and GATS disciplines can in principle be justified under the general exceptions clauses of these agreements (and although considerable deference can be expected to be exercised by WTO panels under these clauses when national energy security is at stake), there is a risk that screening measures may not be justifiable under the Chapeaus, the introductory clauses, of these exceptions. On the other hand, it has been argued in this study that screening measures could in principle more easily be justified under the security exceptions of the GATT and the GATS. However, the scope of application of these security exceptions is narrow, in particular given that they can only be invoked in narrowly defined situations such as in "time of war or emergency in international relations", the existence of which must be objectively determined.[6]

Secondly, as regards the **EU CBAM** mechanism, this study has shown that it is not fully clear whether the CBAM should be regarded as a regulatory internal or a regulatory border measure under WTO law, or whether it is more properly to be classified as a fiscal internal or a fiscal border measure. Depending on this categorization, which has not yet been decided upon in WTO dispute settlement, the CBAM risks violating

[3] Hancher and de Hauteclocque (2024), pp. 61 and 80; and above, Chap. 1.

[4] Cf. above, Chap. 2.

[5] Hancher and de Hauteclocque (2024), p. 56 ff; and above, Chap. 1.

[6] Cf. above, Sect. 4.1.

Art. II:1(b) of the GATT (setting forth upper limits for customs duties and all other duties and charges imposed in connection with importation), Art. III:2 (prohibiting discriminatory fiscal treatment), Art. III:4 (prohibiting discriminatory regulatory measures) and/or Art. XI (prohibiting quantitative restrictions upon importation). Moreover, the CBAM risks infringing the most-favoured-nation clause of the GATT. Although it has been submitted in the literature that various headings of the general exceptions clause of the GATT (Art. XX) could be invoked to justify the CBAM, it seems highly questionable whether the CBAM would also pass scrutiny under the Chapeau of Art. XX. This is due not least to the facts (i) that the CBAM does not make it possible to recognize effective foreign non-price-based climate policies as equivalent to EU measures, (ii) that the CBAM as a unilateral measure is considered to have been adopted without sufficient prior attempts at multilateral negotiations and (iii) that the CBAM does not grant more favourable treatment to developing countries as would be required, however, by WTO and international law.[7]

Thirdly, as respects the **Foreign Subsidies Regulation**, it has been submitted that the WTO Agreement on Subsidies and Countervailing Measures (ASCM), contrary to the view obviously taken by the EU Commission, arguably applies to foreign subsidies. The Foreign Subsidies Regulation therefore risks violating the ASCM, given that the Regulation empowers the EU to take redressive measures and sanctions that are excluded by the *numerus clausus* principle of the ASCM. Furthermore, in contrast to some views held in the literature, the GATS should be regarded as applying to unilateral measures taken under the Foreign Subsidies Regulation, to the extent that such measures affect trade in services and the commercial presence of foreign providers of services. There is a clear risk that such measures could contravene central GATS principles, namely its most-favoured-nation and national treatment clauses. It has been submitted that the EU could try to justify potential violations of the ASCM and the GATS by invoking the general exceptions clauses of the GATT (which should be read as applying to the ASCM, in principle) and the GATS. However, similarly to the Investment Screening Regulation and the CBAM, the Foreign Subsidies Regulation and its application risk violating the Chapeaus of the general exceptions clauses of the GATT and the GATS in substantive as well as procedural terms.[8]

Overall, this study has shown that while it is strategically imperative to protect the EU Internal Energy Market from undue foreign influence in order to promote the EU's "strategic energy autonomy" and its "open strategic autonomy" more generally, it is not an easy task to promote this objective on the basis of unilateral measures such as those analysed in this treatise in a WTO-compliant manner.

Reference

Hancher L, de Hauteclocque A (2024) Strategic autonomy, REPowerEU and the internal energy market: untying the Gordian Knot. Common Mark Law Rev 61(1):55–92

[7] Cf. above, Sect. 4.2.

[8] Cf. Above, Sect. 4.3.

Table of Cases

GATT 1947 and WTO Disputes and Panel Reports

Argentina – Hides and Leather, WT/DS155/R, adopted 16 February 2001, DSR 2001:V, 1779

Brazil – Measures Affecting Imports of Retreaded Tyres, WT/DS332/R, adopted 17 December 2007, as modified by Appellate Body Report WT/DS332/AB/R, DSR 2007:V, p. 1649

Canada – Administration of the Foreign Investment Review Act, L/5504, adopted 7 February 1984, BISD 30S/140 (*Canada – FIRA*)

Canada – Certain Measures Concerning Periodicals, WT/DS31/R, adopted 30 July 1997, DSR 1997:I, 481

Canada — Certain Measures Affecting the Automotive Industry, WT/DS/142/R, adopted on 19 June 2000

European Communities – Regime for the Importation, Sale and Distribution of Bananas, Complaint by the United States, WT/DS27/R/USA, adopted 25 September 1997, as modified by Appellate Body Report WT/DS27/AB/R, DSR 1997:II, 943 *(EC – Bananas III)*

European Communities – Measures Affecting Asbestos and Asbestos-Containing Products, WT/DS135/R and Add.1, adopted 5 April 2001, as modified by Appellate Body Report WT/DS135/AB/R, DSR 2001:VIII, p. 3305

European Communities – Information Technology Products, WT/DS375/R, WT/DS376/R, WT/DS377/R, adopted 21 September 2010, DSR 2010:III, 933

European Union and its Member States – Certain Measures Relating to the Energy Sector, WT/DS476/R, circulated to WTO Members 10 August 2018 [appealed by the European Union on 21 September 2018] (*EU – Energy*)

Panel Report, *Panel on Japanese Measures on Imports of Leather*, 15 May 1984, L/5623

India – Measures Affecting the Automotive Sector, WT/DS146/R, WT/DS175/R, and Corr.1, adopted 5 April 2002, DSR 2002:V, p. 1827

E. Vranes, *EU Energy Politics and WTO Law*, SpringerBriefs in Law,
https://doi.org/10.1007/978-3-032-02392-6

Russia – Measures Concerning Traffic in Transit, WT/DS512/R and Add.1, adopted 26 April 2019, DSR 2019:VIII, 4301 (*Russia – Traffic*)

Saudi Arabia – Measures Concerning the Protection of Intellectual Property Rights, WT/DS567/R and Add.1, circulated to WTO Members on 16 June 2020, dispute terminated while appeal pending (*Saudi Arabia – IPRs*)

Thailand – Customs and Fiscal Measures on Cigarettes from the Philippines, WT/DS371/R, adopted 15 July 2011, as modified by Appellate Body Report WT/DS371/AB/R, DSR 2011:IV, p. 2299

United States – Section 337 of the Tariff Act of 1930, adopted 7 November 1989, L/6439

United States – Measures Affecting Alcoholic and Malt Beverages, adopted on 19 June 1992, DS23/R - 39S/206 (*US – Malt*)

United States – Restrictions on Imports of Tuna, (unadopted) DS21/R – BISD 39S/155, 3 September 1991 (*US – Tuna I*).

United States – Restrictions on Imports of Tuna, DS29/R, 16 June 1994, unadopted

United States – Standards for Reformulated and Conventional Gasoline, WT/DS2/R, adopted 20 May 1996, as modified by Appellate Body Report WT/DS2/AB/R, DSR 1996:I, 29 (*US – Gasoline*)

United States – Tax Treatment for 'Foreign Sales Corporations' (Art. 21.5 DSU), WT/DS/108/R, 8 October 1999

United States – Certain Measures on Steel and Aluminium Products, WT/DS544/R, Add.1 and Suppl.1, circulated to WTO Members 9 December 2022 (*US – Steel (China)*)

United States – Certain Measures on Steel and Aluminium Products, WT/DS552/R, Add.1 and Suppl.1, circulated to WTO Members 9 December 2022 (*US – Steel (Norway)*)

United States – Certain Measures on Steel and Aluminium Products, WT/DS556/R, Add.1 and Suppl.1, circulated to WTO Members 9 December 2022 (*US – Steel (Switzerland)*)

United States – Certain Measures on Steel and Aluminium Products, WT/DS564/R, Add.1 and Suppl.1, circulated to WTO Members 9 December 2022 (*US – Steel (Turkey)*)

United States – Origin Marking Requirement, WT/DS597/R, circulated to Members 21 December 2022

WTO Appellate Body Reports

Brazil – Measures Affecting Imports of Retreaded Tyres, WT/DS332/AB/R, adopted 17 December 2007, DSR 2007:IV, p. 1527 (*Brazil – Retreaded Tyres*),

Canada – Certain Measures Concerning Periodicals, WT/DS31/AB/R, adopted 30 July 1997, DSR 1997:I, p. 449

Canada – Certain Measures Affecting the Renewable Energy Generation Sector and *Canada – Measures Relating to the Feed-In Tariff Program*, AB-2013-1, WT/DS412/AB/R, WT/DS426/AB/R

China – Measures Affecting Imports of Automobile Parts, WT/DS339/AB/R / WT/DS340/AB/R / WT/DS342/AB/R, adopted 12 January 2009, DSR 2009:I, p. 3

China – Measures Related to the Exportation of Various Raw Materials, WT/DS394/AB/R / WT/DS395/AB/R / WT/DS398/AB/R, adopted 22 February 2012, DSR 2012:VII, p. 3295 (*China – Raw Materials*)

China – Measures Related to the Exportation of Rare Earths, Tungsten, and Molybdenum, WT/DS431/AB/R / WT/DS432/AB/R / WT/DS433/AB/R, adopted 29 August 2014, DSR 2014:III, p. 805 (*China – Rare Earths*)

European Communities – Measures Affecting Asbestos and Asbestos-Containing Products, WT/DS135/AB/R, adopted 5 April 2001, DSR 2001:VII, 3243 (*EC – Asbestos*)

European Communities – Seal Products, WT/DS400/AB/R and WT/DS401/AB/R, adopted 18 June 2014, DSR 2014:I, 7

Japan – Taxes on Alcoholic Beverages, WT/DS8/AB/R, WT/DS10/AB/R, WT/DS11/AB/R, adopted 1 November 1996, DSR 1996:I, 97 *(Japan – Alcoholic Beverages II)*

Korea – Measures Affecting Imports of Fresh, Chilled and Frozen Beef, WT/DS161/AB/R, WT/DS169/AB/R, adopted 10 January 2001, DSR 2001:I, 5 (*Korea – Beef*)

United States – Standards for Reformulated and Conventional Gasoline, WT/DS2/AB/R, adopted 20 May 1996, DSR 1996:I, 3 (*US – Gasoline*)

United States – Import Prohibition of Certain Shrimp and Shrimp Products, WT/DS58/AB/R, adopted 6 November 1998, DSR 1998:VII, 2755 (*US – Shrimp*)

United States – Tax Treatment for "Foreign Sales Corporations", WT/DS108/AB/R, adopted 20 March 2000, DSR 2000:III, 1619 (*US – FSC*)

Appellate Body Report, United States – Continued Dumping and Subsidy Offset Act of 2000, WT/DS217/AB/R, WT/DS234/AB/R, adopted 27 January 2003, DSR 2003:I, p. 375

United States – Measures Affecting the Cross-Border Supply of Gambling and Betting Services, WT/DS285/AB/R, adopted 20 April 2005, DSR 2005:XII, p. 5663

Cases Decided by the European Court of Justice

Joined cases C-269/23 P and C-272/23 P, *Hengshi Egypt Fiberglass Fabrics SAE and Jushi Egypt for Fiberglass Industry SAE v European Commission*, ECLI:EU:C:2024:984